Loire

A wine lover's touring guide

Already published:
Alsace
Burgundy
Bordeaux

Forthcoming titles in this series:
Rhône
Provence
Jura/Savoie
Champagne
Languedoc/Roussillon
The Southwest
Corsica

If no address is given for a hotel, park, wine cellar or other place of interest, the reader may assume that everyone in the locality will be able to give directions or that signs point the way.

Hubrecht Duijker

Loire

*A wine lover's
touring guide*

Het Spectrum

Books by Het Spectrum are brought onto the market by:
Publishing House Het Spectrum B.V.
Postbus 2073
3500 GB Utrecht
The Netherlands

The author will be grateful for any suggestions, ideas and comments concerning this guide.
You may send them to the above address, attn. Hubrecht Duijker.

Copyright © 1994 by Hubrecht Duijker
Cover design: Alpha Design, Leusden, The Netherlands
Photos: Hubrecht Duijker
Translation: Paul Goodman
Lay out/Typesetting: Meijster Design, Haarlem, The Netherlands
Lithography: RCA, Zwolle, The Netherlands
Cartography: Autorisation IGN n° 90-4007.
TOP 250 n° 106 © IGN Paris 1992
TOP 250 n° 108 © IGN Paris 1994
Carte de France des vins et eaux de vie d'appellation d'origine - © Reproduction interdite -
Tous droits réservés Editions Benoit France.
Printing: Aubin Imprimeur, Ligugé, France
First edition: 1994

Cover photo: Beautiful Candes-Saint-Martin, which lies at the point where the Loire and
Vienne flow together.

This edition © 1994 by Het Spectrum B.V

ISBN 1-85365-331-4

British Library Cataloguing-in-Publication Data.
A catalogue record for this book is available from the British Library.

Contents

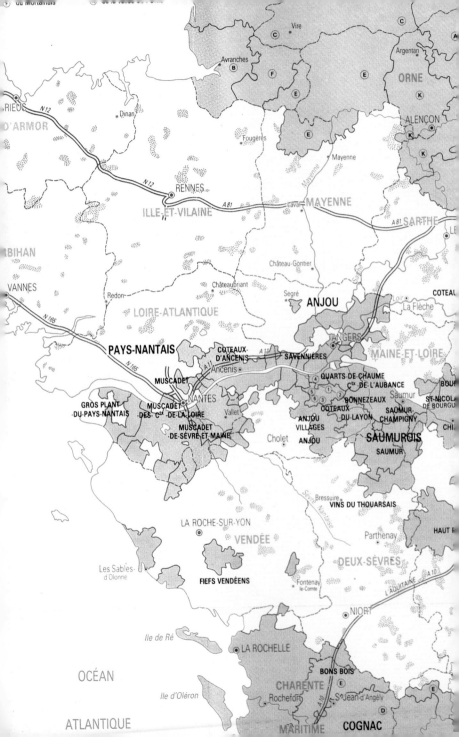

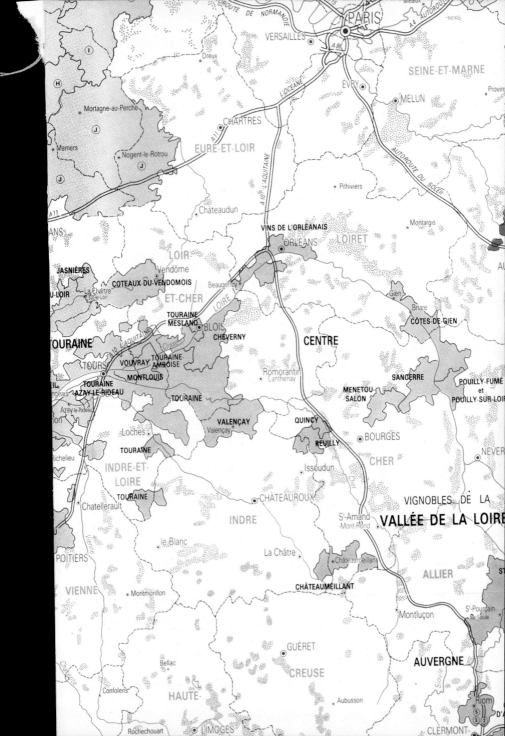

An Introduction to the Loire

The River Loire rises as an unimportant rill in a volcanic mountain range to the southeast of Le Puy in the Massif Central. Its source is situated at a height of 1,400 metres, below a volcanic upthrust of the Gerbier de Jonc and at the junction of two departmental routes. At first the river tumbles and foams in a southerly direction through mountain gorges and, in so doing, threatens to merge with the nearby and powerful Rhône. Then, after about 10 kilometres, the river suddenly alters its course in a westerly, and afterwards northerly, direction, impeded by the massif of the 1,471-metre-high Suc de Bardon. Shortly thereafter an artificial lake is created by La Palisse reservoir. The Loire then continues its tortuous journey at full speed, through Le Puy and the impressive *gorges* a few dozen kilometres north of the industrial city of Saint-Etienne, where the erosive power of the water has created deep ravines. In the neighbourhood of Roanne – almost as well known for the *Troisgros* restaurant as for its Michelin tyre factory – the first grapevines begin to appear. The small wine area of Côte Roannaise is situated just west of the city. Further to the west runs the Allier, which follows the course of the Loire for about 400 kilometres before merging with it near Nevers. It is here that the Loire becomes a truly powerful river. About 40 kilometres further on is the first important wine area, Pouilly-Fumé, and, diagonally across from it, the hill on which the wine village of Sancerre stands. The river now runs in a northwesterly direction. Its northernmost point is Orléans, where it sweeps gracefully in a southwesterly direction to flow by way of Blois, Tours, Angers and Nantes into the Atlantic Ocean. By then the river has travelled 1,012 kilometres solely within France itself. This is approximately 200 kilometres longer than the Rhône which actually originates in Switzerland. During its journey through France, the Loire crosses no fewer than 12 departments. Along the way it is fed by the waters of countless tributaries, among them the Allier, Arroux, Cher, Erdre, Indre, Moine, Nièvre and Vienne. The Loire basin covers about one-fifth of the entire country, making it the most French of all rivers. The other rivers of France can be considered regional; the Loire, on the contrary, is truly national. Starting at Nevers, the appearance of the river undergoes a metamorphosis. Steep, spectacular banks, sharp bends and tempestuous water make way for a much more peaceful and sedate flow. The lively princess becomes a circumspect queen and the Loire flows through France in harmony with its surroundings. Almost everywhere the banks are low and the bends wide. Thanks to its many tributaries, it is well fed, becoming broader and broader, while the silt that is carried along turns the water brown. The Loire is at its most powerful from late autumn to early spring when it swells with rain and melted snow water to fill its entire bed. Then it may temporarily lose its good nature and become a threat to everything in or near its path. It is not by chance that Henry II Plantagenet (12th century) ordered dikes to be built to protect villages, cities and estates along its path. This was the beginning of a centuries-long creation of a water-regulating network of dams, basins and canals. In spite of this, floods still took place now and then, as in 1856. Those who have seen the Loire at its fullest can scarcely imagine how much it slims down in the warm season, not to mention a really dry summer. The Loire is then a mere shadow of itself, and large sections of the river are no longer navigable. In earlier times this would have been disastrous because, for hundreds of years, the river served as France's main trade route. All

Portal of the cathedral in Bourges.

sorts of wares were transported in flat-bottomed boats and special authorities saw to it that not only was the channel kept free but also the towpaths as, during a headwind, many boats were towed. Unwelcome visitors also arrived by means of the waterway, such as the plundering Vikings, who, in the 9th century, penetrated as far as Orléans. Among the goods transported down the Loire was wine, the Dutch then being the greatest foreign customers. In the Muscadet area (near Nantes) the Dutch began to encourage the planting of white grape varieties, the purpose of which was to produce a light wine for distillation. Previously, they had obtained such a wine from Charente, but taxes had become too high there. In 1646 a merchant from Nantes noted: 'The Dutch have introduced a certain custom whereby the wines are bottled, transferred to another cask, sulphurised and strengthened, by which means they can be conserved better during transportation and can be sold in the northern countries.' One of the grapes that the Dutch introduced was the folle blanche, from which Gros Plant du Pays Nantais is now made. Dutch influence was also strong further up the river. In Anjou they bought sweet white wines for table use, and in the 16th and 17th centuries Anjou's entire wine-trade was monopolised by the Dutch, with the Loire, of course, still serving as the route to the sea. In the 18th century much wine was still being shipped down the Loire. The account book of a merchant of Saint-Thibault (a river village near Sancerre) mentions that, in 1820, 4,340 casks (*pièces*) per ship were sent, at a value of 4,340,000 gold francs. Just how busy the inland shipping trade still was in the first half of the last century is shown by the fact that, in 1834, to the southeast of Orléans alone, more than 19,000 flat-bottomed boats were in use. Well over a decade later, the steam locomotive made its appearance, which signalled the end of the Loire shipping trade. Nowadays even pleasure yachts prefer to use the side canals.

Bridge over the Loire at Beaugency.

The Loire valley is at its most beautiful in May and June, when the foliage is fresh and the flowers are in bloom. In the second half of May, for example, 25,000 irises flower in the Parc Floral Source de Loiret near Orléans and in the second half of June 100,000 rose bushes are in full blossom. In other parts of the valley there are azaleas, camelias, chrysanthemums, hydrangeas, magnolias and rhododendrons. Numerous fruit trees also blossom. This 'garden of France' produces many apples, pears, cherries and plums, while the soil and climate encourage the cultivation of strawberries, raspberries, currants, melons, blackberries, nuts and, of course, wine grapes. In the summer and early autumn, the Loire is unusually attractive. The leaves of deciduous trees and grapevines shine with a golden glow, while the softer sunlight makes the contours of hills and buildings less sharp in outline.

The most important attractions of the Loire valley are really not the landscape nor the wine but the castles. It is said that: 'The Loire is a queen and kings have loved her' because, for reasons of politics and pleasure, French noblemen and other wealthy rulers once built marvellous castles along the Loire and its tributaries. The great period of castle building started in 1453 after the English had been permanently driven from France. In the beginning, these fortresses had a military character but they soon acquired the appearance of lovely mansions. Above all, the French Renaissance style blossomed here. Sobriety and strictly prescribed proportions gave way to a richly decorative style in which Italian influences could be clearly seen. It is not by chance that Francis I demonstrated his affinity with Italy by convincing Leonardo da Vinci to come to Amboise in 1516. The most beautiful examples of Renaissance castles are found in Touraine and its surroundings, while elsewhere in this impressive valley visits to wine districts, wine villages and cellars can be combined with the many visual pleasures offered by the castles. You can also enjoy architectural works of art in other styles and forms, such as cathedrals, churches, chapels, mansions, bridges, statues and fountains. 'The Loire valley', wrote Michelet, 'is a monk's habit with golden trimmings.'

Not only wine but also fruit.

Historical Perspective

The history of the Loire is closely tied to that of the whole of France, because the French nation was actually born in the Loire valley and many kings established their centres of government here. Reminders of the earliest inhabitants, those of the Neolithic Age, are still present in the form of dolmens: stone tables made out of enormous rocks. They date from about 2500 BC. Excavated tools, from this and later periods, can be found in museums all along the Loire. Between 1200 and 400 BC the Celts came to the area, where they established important settlements. The names of some of the tribes can still be heard in the placenames. Nantes, for example, was founded by the Namnets, Bourges by the Biturgs and Tours by the Turones. In 58 BC Julius Caesar invaded and conquered Gaul. Six years later a revolt

The impressive Château de Chambord.

began in the city we know as Orléans and was bloodily snuffed out by Caesar. In about the year AD 250 Christianity was introduced under the leadership of Saint Gatien, the first archbishop of Tours. The same city received Martinus as archbishop in the 4th century. At the beginning of that century, Constantine the Great had already made Christianity the official religion of the Roman Empire but at that time it had only reached the cities, not the rural areas. Martinus changed this, not only in Touraine but also in Anjou and other areas. In 361, he founded the first French monastery. After his death, in 397, he became one of France's most revered saints. Almost 500 communities are named after him and more than 3,500 churches.

With the fall of the Roman Empire, Gaul experienced invasions by the Franks, Huns and Visigoths. The Huns were defeated and, in 504, the Frankish King Clovis and the Visigoth King Alarik signed a peace treaty near Amboise. This was not the end of skirmishes, however,

Wall-hanging in the castle of Cheverny.

because three years later the Visigoths were driven over the Pyrenees. Following the Frankish house of the Merovingians, the Carolingians came to power in 752 (including, among others, Charlemagne, who ruled from 771-814). When this dynasty died out, power was transferred to Hugh Capet in 987, who was followed by 14 descendants, the Capetians. Under their regime – and thanks to many well-arranged marriages – their empire (Anjou) continued to grow until it covered about half of present-day France. In 1154 Henry II Plantagenet became ruler of both Anjou and England. He often stayed at Chinon and also died there in 1189. The fact that a great deal of France came under English rule, and that the English continued to claim the French throne, was a direct cause of the Hundred Years War (1137-1453). It was Joan of Arc who, in 1429, was able to break the English siege of Orléans, which marked the beginning of the English retreat from the Loire area and the rest of France. Before she was burnt in 1431, Joan convinced Charles VII (of the house of Valois, which had reigned since 1328), who doubted his birthright, to crown himself at Reims. His son Louis XI finally defeated the English and held court at Tours, which also became the French capital. Under Charles VIII Brittany was added to the empire, thanks to his marriage to 15-year-old Anne of Brittany in 1491. His successor, Louis XII, also married Anne, eight years later, and her daughter later married Francis of Angoulème, who, in 1515, ascended the throne as Francis I. Under his rule and that of his two predecessors, the Loire area experienced its heyday. The kings and other wealthy rulers built wonderous castles, often with the help of Italian architects or strongly influenced by the Italian style. The Renaissance began in the reign of Francis I, which lasted until 1547. Among the castles of this period are, entirely or in part, Azay-le-Rideau, Beauregard, Blois, Chambord, Chaumont, Chenonceau, Ussé, Valençay and Villandry. Francis I was succeeded by

Henry II – who took the same mistress as Francis, Diane de Poitiers. Directly after Henry's death, in 1559, Catherine de Médicis, Henry's wife, banned his mistress from her beloved Chenonceau and became regent with well-nigh absolute power. During the second half of the 16th century the Loire area was the scene of religious wars. Under Charles IX and HenryIII violent confrontations took place between Catholics and Protestants. The end came in 1589, when Henry IV took the throne as the first of the Bourbons. This epicurean, born in Pau, signed the Edict of Nantes, which gave the Huguenots freedom of religion and ended the war. In order to become king, Henry had to convert to Catholicism, saying: 'Paris is worth a mass to me.' The government was also finally established in Paris and neighbouring Versailles. From that moment on, the Loire region began to lose political weight and, as a result, was no longer a place where the nobility settled. What did develop was trade, and, as the Loire became the country's most important traffic route, all types of industries established themselves along the river, with Protestants playing no small role. The revocation of the Edict of Nantes (1685) was disastrous for the area, because countless Huguenots were forced to flee and the regional economy mostly collapsed. It was Louis XIV, the Sun King and builder of the new palace at Versailles, who put an end to freedom of religion. Violent fighting took place in the Loire region once again, in 1793, when a peasant army from the Vendée (south of Nantes), which was loyal to the king, clashed with the revolutionaries. Reminders of this revolt can be found in the museum at the castle in Nantes. Almost 90 of the peasants who died were later canonised. During the Second World War great destruction occurred in many of the Loire cities, such as Amboise, Angers, Nantes, Orléans and Tours. Many historical buildings and districts have since been restored with great care, so that visitors to this valley, which is so rich in history, can enjoy this unique architectural heritage to the full.

VITICULTURE AND WINES

If one imagined the Loire as the edge of a giant artist's palette and could choose a different colour for each of the wine areas, not only would a good collection of strong colours be seen, but also many shades in between because several areas overlap with each other, which means that the producers can make many sorts of wines with various appellations. Around Nantes you can taste two types of Muscadet made by many small farmers and, in the surroundings of Pouilly-sur-Loire, the same number of Pouilly-Fumés. Along the Layon river to the south of Angers, on the same estate, several types of Coteaux du Layon, a Quarts de Chaume, white Anjou, red Anjou and one or two types of Rosé d'Anjou are found. This alone shows that, among over 30 Loire wine areas, large differences exist. All the areas lie within the Loire basin, although the distances between some of the wine areas and France's largest river are sometimes considerable. Thus Valençay is situated some 40 kilometres from the nearest Loire bank and Reuilly almost 80. Considering the area over which they are spread, therefore, it is not

Winegrower tasting his cabernet-franc.

so surprising that differences exist between the wine districts. As the crow flies, it is almost 350 kilometres from Nantes, near the Atlantic Ocean, to Pouilly-sur-Loire – and if you follow the course of the Loire it is much more. Obviously Nantes has a different climate to that found further inland and there also exist geographical and geological contrasts, not to mention the differences in history, cuisine and tradition. This diversity in natural and human factors has resulted in the cultivation of a large range of grape varieties. It is often asserted that the Loire region mainly produces fresh, dry white wines. This holds for a few areas but certainly not for all of them. Quite large quantities of medium-dry and sweet whites wines are produced, along with millions of bottles of sparkling wine. Aside from this, the region offers various types of rosé, varying from the famous semi-sweet Rosé d'Anjou to the dry Rosé de Loire, the rather rare Sancerre rosé and Reuilly rosé, coming from the pinot noir and pinot gris grapes, respectively. Last but not least are the red wines, which are very varied in character. You will find Beaujolais-like Gamays, red Cabernets which remind one of Bordeaux, Pinots Noirs with the taste of a minor Bourgogne, and all possible sorts in between. Because the Loire valley is not dominated by a high mountain chain, the tempering influence of the westerly sea wind is noticeable deep inland, and therefore a rather mild climate, without extreme temperatures, exists. This is ideal for winegrowing. Only now and then is the region forced to contend with night-frost, as in 1991, when a large part of the harvest was lost in

Wine landscape at Reuilly.

many of the wine areas. In the Loire area it becomes less warm than in the more southern areas, such as Bordeaux and the Rhône valley, or in Burgundy where an inland climate predominates. This means that black grapes will be generally somewhat less ripe and rich in sugar, which results in lighter wines, with less roundness, flesh and alcohol. This does not deny the fact that there are red Loire wines – such as certain Chinons – with sufficient extract and tannin to ripen for years. In general, however, the white grapes mature without problems. They are sometimes picked intentionally early – as in Muscadet, where they strive for wines as light as a feather with a spring-like freshness – but sometimes also very late, even into November. This happens in areas where sweet white wine is one of the specialities, such as Coteaux du Layon. There, overripe grapes are sought, preferably affected by 'noble rot', when thanks to the variation between misty mornings and sunny afternoons, the fruits are affected by a benevolent mould. As a result of this, the grapes dry out in part, while, at the same time, the aroma of

In Chavignol (Sancerre).

the flesh undergoes a change. Because this process of *pourriture noble* works irregularly, however, pickers have to go through the vineyard several times in order to pick only the really affected grapes. In other areas the drone, hum and rattle of picking machines dominates harvest time but in Coteaux du Layon and similar areas small groups of pickers walk patiently along the rows of vines.

Since prehistoric times the Loire has swept along sand, pebbles, clay and other soil elements and in many of the wine areas of its basin the soil is characterised by differing compositions of these elements. In some places, however, lime is also found in the soil. In Reuilly the soil is very similar to that of Chablis, while elsewhere a thick layer of tufa stone is present. Concentrations of this soft, marl-like limestone are found above all in Touraine, for example in the areas of Saumur and Vouvray. The grapes thrive to perfection on this soil. The stone itself was formerly much in demand for building houses, churches and castles, so many tunnels exist. Nowadays these serve as storage cellars for wine or the cultivation of mushrooms. In former times complete houses were carved out of the sides of the tufa stone layer. Some are still occupied. In Rochecorbon, near Vouvray, there is even a luxury hotel with cave rooms. The same area also has a few restaurants situated in caves. The tufa stone of Touraine is quite hard. A softer variety is found in the region of Sancerre, for example near Bué. A soil type also exists here called *caillotes*: a combination of soft, porous tufa stone and small pebbles. This stone is too soft to excavate caves. While Bordeaux is characterised by relatively widespread estates, and Burgundy by small ones, most of the estates in the Loire valley are small to medium-sized. A wine estate of 30 to 40 hectares is regarded as really big. There are also large numbers of farmers who work less than 10 hectares. Many winegrowers vinify their own wine and put it onto the market in bottled form. Others work closely with a wine merchant or are members of a co-operative. A few of the most important *négociants* are situated in Saint-Hilaire-Saint-Florent, a neighbouring community of Saumur. Elsewhere the wine houses are also very active, as in Muscadet and Touraine. In a few areas the majority of the wine is produced by co-operatives. This is the case, for example, in Coteaux d'Ancenis and the Orléanais. In some places, however, co-operatives do not exist or are few: collectivity is not very popular in the 'red' areas of Bourgueil, Saint-Nicolas-de-Bourgueil and Chinon.

In the descriptions of the wine areas and their wines in this guide, grape varieties are often named. This is because they determine, to a

Richelieu, immortalised in Amboise.

large extent, the sorts of wine that the region in question makes, as well as the character of the wines. In order to understand the wines of the Loire valley, it is important to be acquainted with the grape varieties. For this reason, there follows, in alphabetical order, a list of the most common white and black grapes.

WHITE GRAPE VARIETIES
Chardonnay Originally from Burgundy but nowadays planted more and more in the Loire region. Pure Chardonnay is seldom encountered, or at any rate with an appellation contrôlée. Much Chardonnay is brought out as Vin de Pays du Jardin de la France. One of the rare areas to produce pure Chardonnay is the Orléanais. The grape variety is difficult to recognise there, however, because, locally, it is called auvernat blanc. The grape names are given in this book in lower case (e.g. cabernet sauvignon); the wines in upper case (Cabernet Sauvignon). Sparse amounts of pure Chardonnay are produced in areas such as Cheverny and Valençay. In other regions chardonnay is mixed with chenin blanc, usually to a maximum of 20 per cent. This is the case in Anjou and Saumur. Characteristic of the chardonnay is an aroma of tropical fruits, such as mango and passion fruit.

Chenin blanc or *pineau de la Loire* This is the most characteristic of all Loire grapes. It has its origins in this valley and is the base grape for a large number of white wines. Included among these are white Anjou,

Wine shop in Sancerre.

Coteaux de l'Aubance, Coteaux du Layon, Montlouis, Saumur, Savennières, certain types of Touraine and Vouvray. A striking aspect of the chenin blanc is its versatility. The grape can be used for very dry wines as well as almost luxuriously sweet ones – with all variants in between. What's more, it lends itself to be worked into sparkling or slightly sparkling wines (*pétillant*). In the aroma of a chenin wine there is often something of apple and pear, together with a touch of spices but, above all in the sweet wines, other nuances can be present. Good chenin wines can also ripen a long time, sometimes for decades.

Gros plant or *folle blanche* A productive, simple variety which gives a rather acidic wine of little distinction. In the neighbourhood of Nantes they make a Gros Plant du Pays Nantais from it. The wine tastes at its best with seafood such as mussels. In the southwest of France a light wine from the same grape is distilled.

Muscadet or *melon de Bourgogne* The only base grape for all Muscadet. It is quite frost-resistant, which is partially the reason it was brought to the area centuries ago. It gives a dry white wine with relatively little alcohol, but one that is refreshing but low in acid. Muscadet complements all sorts of fish dishes, as well as crustaceans and shellfish. What's more, this slightly sparkling wine makes a good apéritif.

Pinot Gris or *malvoisie* A not very productive variety which is rather vulnerable. Several wines are made from it, which vary from semi-sweet white (for example Coteaux d'Ancenis) to pale, dry rosés (Reuilly).

Romorantin A typical Loire grape which grows almost only in Cheverny. The wine made from it is very lively and dry with an unusual floral aroma and ripening potential.

Sauvignon blanc This is the base grape for the well-known white wines of the upper Loire, Pouilly-Fumé and Sancerre. In other less well-known areas, however, it is also an important variety, as in Menetou-Salon, Quincy and Reuilly, while, within the appellation Touraine much Sauvignon is produced. Loire wines from the sauvignon are usually characterised by a radiating bouquet in which the aroma of the fruit (above all that of gooseberries) as well as something vegetable-like (asparagus, fennel, grass) can be present, while you can also often discover a floral quality (in the form of violets and spring flowers). In some Loire regions the sauvignon plays a minor role, as in Anjou, Cheverny, Coteaux du Giennois and Saumur.

BLACK GRAPE VARIETIES

Cabernet franc or *breton* A variety that originated in Bordeaux and is a close relative of the cabernet sauvignon but gives somewhat gentler

wines, aromatic, less refined and supplied with much tannin. Certain red Loire wines from the cabernet franc can ripen excellently, such as Bourgueil and Chinon. There are also wines that actually age relatively quickly

Clos Saint Fiacre (Orléanais) has a small museum.

– also in this case the soil in which the vines grow plays an important role in determining the personality of the wine. The cabernet franc is present almost everywhere that red wine is made in Anjou and Touraine. Within the appellation Touraine it is usually blended with other varieties. In Anjou it forms the base for the semi-dry Cabernet d'Anjou rosé.

Cabernet sauvignon This is another classic grape from Bordeaux. The wines made from it have more distinction and refinement than those of the cabernet franc, and in their youth they frequently have an aroma of blackcurrants. In the Loire valley the cabernet sauvignon is less successful than it is in Bordeaux, which has to do with the northerly location of this area and is why a pure Cabernet Sauvignon is seldom encountered. The variety is mainly used in blends.

Gamay This grape – the base of all red Beaujolais – does very well in the Loire valley. Here, its wines are often similar to Beaujolais, with that very characteristic aroma of small red fruits and berries (strawberries, raspberries, cherries, etc.), although they can taste somewhat less supple. A portion of the gamay harvest is worked into primeur wines. A number of producers mix the gamay with other varieties, frequently the cabernet franc. This can lead to very successful results. The gamay is very common in Anjou and Touraine, although it is found only on a modest scale in small areas such as Coteaux d'Ancenis and Coteaux du Giennois (west and east in the valley, respectively).

Groslot or *grolleau* A rather simple Loire grape that is mainly used for making semi-dry Rosé d'Anjou.

Malbec or *cot* A grape variety from Bordeaux. It gives rather colourful wines with a lot of tannin. In some areas surprisingly good wines are made from it, for example in Touraine-Amboise, Cheverny and Valençay, while elsewhere it is generally cultivated in order to be mixed, as within the area of Touraine.

Pineau d'Aunis or *chenin noir* This is an original Loire grape (Aunis is a village in the area around Saumur) which gives fresh, dry rosés and, in a few cases, red wines also. Just like various other varieties of white and black grapes, it can serve as a base for sparkling Saumur Brut or Crémant de Loire.

Pinot noir In Burgundy all the better wines are made from this grape. For decades the product of this grape has not been especially good in the Loire valley but nowadays serious producers are more and more often able to make delicious wines from it, both red and rosé. Examples will be found in Menetou-Salon and Sancerre. The best wines mature in oak casks. In the Orléanais the pinot noir is frequently called auvernat rouge.

The Cuisine

Travelling along the Loire not only means enjoying the scenery, villages, cities, castles and wines but also the many aromas and tastes that the region's gastronomy has to offer. The age-long presence of royal households encouraged local gastronomy to flourish and it still does today. In Muscadet, near the Loire estuary, much seafood is eaten. Oysters are frequently on the menu, as well as mussels. *Moules* are served in various ways. At meals out of doors they are laid on large platters and covered with twigs or straw, which is then set on fire. In this way the mussels are cooked and smoked at the same time. In Muscadet fresh sea fish are often eaten and also a lot of freshwater fish – this holds true for the whole valley. In the Loire basin there are numerous rivers, streams and lakes where fish are bred and caught. Among these are pike *brochet*, often served in *quenelles*, small, creamy 'custards', pike perch (*sandre*), shad (*alose*) and eel (*anguille*). Crayfish (*écrevisses*) are also often served, as are *friture* (small fried fish, which you eat whole). Loire salmon exist but they are extraordinarily scarce. The fish are prepared in all possible ways, frequently with a sauce in which the local wine is used. The most famous fish sauce is *beurre blanc*, a creamy combination of butter, shallots and vinegar or white wine. The Loire valley also has much to offer in the way of meat. Pork is the most important type. In Touraine and Anjou the rather fatty parts of the pig are made into *rillettes*, small pieces of meat which are salted, left to simmer for a few hours and thereafter cut into strips then covered with fat. Served on toast or bread *rillettes* form a delicious first course, accompanied, for example, by a dry Vouvray Pétillant. There are also *rillons*. These are pieces of meat which have been prepared in the same way, although not made into strips, and fried briefly until they are crisp. *Rillauds* or *rillots* come from Anjou and are comparable to *rillettes*, although caramel is added and the dish is served warm instead of cold. Pork is also made into ham, as in the area of Sancerre, where smoked *jambon de Sancerre* can frequently be ordered. *Pruneaux*, dried plums, are a popular ingredient with pork.

One of the reasons why the French monarchs loved to stay in the Loire area was the possibility of hunting. Hunting is still very popular here, which results in many game dishes appearing on restaurant menus in season. Among these are quail (*caille*), hare (*lièvre*), partridge (*perdreau*), rabbit (*lapin*), young rabbit (*lapereau*) and wild boar (*sanglier*). Fowl is also popular – note the numerous times that *coq au vin* appears on menus.

Vegetable lovers will enjoy themselves immensely in the Loire valley, where great amounts of vegetables are produced. Asparagus from Touraine has the place of honour, and can be combined perfectly with white wines such as Sauvignon Touraine, Sancerre, Pouilly-Fumé, Menetou-Salon, Quincy and Reuilly. Other popular vegetables are artichokes, cauliflowers and all sorts of other brassicas, cucumbers, leeks, radishes, shallots, lettuce, tomatoes, onions and fennel.

Fruit is also plentiful as orchards can be found everywhere in the valley. These produce apples and pears as well as cherries, melons, strawberries and blackberries. In restaurants fruits are used in all

At dinner in Azay-le-Rideau.

sorts of pies. One of France's most famous is the *tarte tatin*, an upside-down, caramelised apple pie. This creation was named after the Tatin *demoiselles* who ran a restaurant in Lamotte-Beuvron, a village 35 kilometres south of Orléans. The restaurant (also a hotel), across from the station, still exists. Other delicacies are *crêpes* (often filled with fruit) and butter biscuits from the area around Nantes, as well as chocolate cake from Blois. The most characteristic cheeses are made from goat's milk. The Crottin de Chavignol, which has its own appellation, is very famous. The cheese is very small and its crust becomes darker the longer it ripens, thus the not-so-flattering name of *crottin* which means horse dung. Crottin de Chavignol (cold or warm) tastes well-nigh perfect with white Sancerre. Chavignol is in fact a wine village in the Sancerre region. Other well-known goat cheeses are those of Selles-sur-Cher (soft-tasting and covered with charcoal powder; it is also called Romorantin) and Valençay (pithy taste and pyramid-shaped). A renowned cow's milk cheese is the blue-veined Olivet.

How to Use this Guide

This guide will lead you through almost all of the wine areas of the Loire and its tributaries, all the way from the sea, where the Muscadet region is situated, hundreds of kilometres inland to the areas of Sancerre and Pouilly-Fumé. In almost every chapter a route is picked out that runs by the most interesting wine villages and the most beautiful scenery, while much attention has also been paid to the numerous castles of the Loire valley. The most important places of interest and other tourist aspects are covered in each district. Where possible, hotels and restaurants are recommended, always with price indications. In principle, hotel prices are for a double room without breakfast. Several restaurants and some of the hotels will be found in no other guide. These are usually small, cosy, rural places where you can enjoy a pleasant stay at reasonable prices. The best wine producers are also mentioned in each area, sometimes with one or more of their best wines. This selection is one of the most complete ever made for the Loire. Finally, there are separate chapters devoted to the cities of Angers, Blois, Bourges, Nantes, Orléans and Tours. They are not actually wine cities, but really do deserve a visit if you are in the neighbouring wine areas.

Hotels
When reserving a hotel room, always ask for a peacefully situated room, at the rear or next to a courtyard if possible. Watch out for loud and frequently rung church bells. At the time of reservation, you will be informed of a final arrival time. If you intend arriving later, you are advised to telephone, otherwise there is a chance that your room will be given away. Written confirmation of a reservation is also wise. Do this by letter or fax (having asked for the number). As elsewhere in France, *gîtes* or *chambres d'hôte* may be rented privately in the Loire area. There is often a list of addresses at the town hall or at the *bureau* or *office du tourisme.*

Restaurants
It is very wise to telephone restaurants in advance, on the one hand to be sure of a table, and on the other to verify that the establishment is open on that particular day. Experience has shown that it is sensible mainly to order one of the suggested menus because they are generally cheaper. They often contain market-fresh ingredients. In simple

eating-houses it is best to choose regional dishes because the chef will probably struggle with complex and expensive recipes from elsewhere. Always choose regional wines and, if possible, wines from the village itself, because they will have been chosen with more expertise and care than wines from other areas. A carafe of water is always free but mineral water can also be ordered.

WINEGROWERS
It may take a lot of effort to arrange a visit to famous winegrowers, especially if they can sell their wines without problems for a lot of money. There are also quite a few wine-producing castles that state clearly that visitors are not welcome. Don't give up too quickly, however, because if you are really interested in wine – and show it – most doors will eventually open for you. It can also help to show them this guide: someone who comes by recommendation and also appears to be truly interested in wines is usually more pleasantly received than a passing stranger. When tasting the wines – which can vary from one or two in the

Wine can be tasted throughout the valley.

Muscadet to a whole range in Anjou – it is normal to spit them out but ask first where you can do this. Also ask what you must do with any remainder in the glass, because the producer sometimes has a special container for it. Never offer the winegrower a tip but do buy at least one bottle as a token of your appreciation of the hospitality enjoyed. In general, French is the means of communication, although many young winegrowers now speak English.

Le Pays Nantais

The western wine area of the Loire makes an excellent starting point for a trip through the valley of France's longest river – although it makes an equally good finish. While elsewhere along the Loire you mainly step back in time – by visiting old villages, cities, churches and castles – Nantes, the most important city of the western region, offers a 20th-century viewpoint. Certainly, there are monuments that are hundreds of years old, such as the castle and cathedral, but they play a minor role in the image of this harbour city. Nantes is not the only place that holds an exceptional position when compared to other Loire cities, the same holds true for the surrounding landscape, Le Pays Nantais. The climate here is more maritime then anywhere else along the Loire, with more rain and a frequent westerly wind which blows the sky clean and clear. The sky of Le Pays Nantais, with its nimble white clouds against a fresh blue backdrop reminds one of the light that the early Dutch masters captured in their paintings. Despite the influence of the nearby ocean, the type of weather that prevails here is seldom severe and generally mild. In the heart of the most prominent wine area, Muscadet, magnolias, fig trees, laurels, cedars and some-times even Mediterranean pine trees grow, which means that grape-vines also thrive without problems. It very seldom freezes so hard that the harvest is lost and the wine vines fail (in 1991 the area was hit hard by a disastrous cold spell, the same fate that befell the other French regions). Another factor that differentiates Le Pays Nantais from the other Loire regions is the grapes – varieties are cultivated here that can be found nowhere else. Thus, all Muscadet is made from the muscadet or melon de Bourgogne. For the wine of the area with the second largest volume, Gros Plant du Pays Nantais, the folle blanche is planted. Both wines are excellent with all sorts of seafood, which this region supplies in large amounts. Finally, the region around Nantes has its own historical character. Until the 15th century the dukes of the independent duchy of Brittany ruled here, not the kings of France.

NANTES

Numbered among the famous people born in Nantes, France's seventh city, are Phileas Fogg, Captain Nemo and Michael Strogoff, all characters from the novels of Jules Verne. This imaginative author (1828-1905) is a son of Nantes and wrote some of his best-known books here. Nantes has a museum devoted to him that contains all sorts of items concerning Verne and his work. Near the museum is a planetarium, which is also open to the public (3, rue de l'Hermitage). That the imagination of Jules Verne was particularly stimulated in Nantes may be attributed to the character of this city, because Nantes has been an important port for centuries. One can imagine Jules Verne wandering along the docks, where foreign sailors unloaded tropical goods from Africa and the French colonies in the Caribbean. Nantes, which was named after the tribe of the Namnets, was an important trading centre in Roman times. In the Middle Ages it became the principal seat of the dukes of Brittany. Between the 10th and 15th centuries the city experienced its heyday. In 1466 duke Francis II rebuilt the local castle as a powerful stronghold with round turrets at the corners. It is somewhat like the castle of Angers but on a smaller scale. In 1468 Duke Francis signed a treaty with Louis XI of France, which paved the way for Brittany to become part of the French empire. None the less, when Francis II died in 1488, a French army under the command of Charles VIII appeared in front of the castle. The purpose of this expedition was to pay court to the 11-year-old heiress to the Breton duchy, Anne of Breton. She did, indeed, marry Charles VIII and later also Louis XII but these were not happy marriages for her. The castle formerly stood on a tributary of the Loire but now it is surrounded by streets and a square. Three museums are housed inside the impressive, rather gloomy-looking building. In one of the towers is the Musée des Arts Décoratifs, with arts and crafts (above all, textiles). In the main building the Musée des Arts Populaires is established, which displays many aspects of Breton folk art. The Musée des Salorges, on the east side of the castle, is devoted to the history of shipping and trade in Nantes. The ducal castle was also where Henry IV signed the Edict of Nantes in 1598, which gave freedom of religion to the Protestants – until it was revoked in 1685. It may be an idea to leave your car by the castle, because most other places of interest are within walking distance. The cathedral of Saint-Pierre-et-Saint-Paul was worked on for about four centuries. It

remains a truly Gothic building, as is seen by the three-part portal.
The church has a marvellous organ but still more impressive is the
richly decorated monument to Francis II. The Saint-Pierre gate, on the
square at the north side of the cathedral, is a former 14th-century city
gate with a Gallic-Romanic foundation. The Musée des Beaux-Arts
(rue Clémenceau) contains a wide collection of paintings from various
countries and periods. Included are Italian primitives and works from
the school of Barbizon. Near to the museum is the Jardin des Plantes.
Here a statue of Jules Verne is encircled by a large collection of tropical
plants, the seeds of which were brought back by captains in the
shipping trade. In the garden the
oldest magnolia in Europe grows.
Another interesting garden is
found at the west side of the
castle. The former Ile Feydeau
(between the cour F. Roosevelt
and the allée Turenne) shows the
prosperous Nantes of earlier
times. By walking in a northerly
direction, by way of the place du
Commerce, you can reach the

The local castle.

famous Passage Pommeraye. This is a covered shopping arcade from
the last century, with wrought-iron balustrades, white pillars and
dozens of statuettes. Further west are three more museums but on the
way don't forget to drop into the *Brasserie La Cigale*, a marvellously
decorated restaurant with colourful mosaics in fin de siècle style (place
Graslin, across from the theatre). The Musée d'Histoire Naturelle
exhibits flora and fauna from the whole world (thanks to shipping),
the Musée Archéologique brings the far past to life by means of
excavated objects and utensils and the Musée Dobrée displays a wide
range of art from a private collection. Next door, the Palais Dobrée is
devoted, among other things, to the history of the Vendée. Finally, in
summer it is possible to take a boat trip (with a meal on board) along
the Erdre river, once called 'the most beautiful river of France' by
François I.

HOTELS
Abbaye de Villeneuve
Les Sorinières
☎ 40.04.40.25
An 18th-century
monastery which now
functions as an
unusually comfortable
and peaceful hotel, just
south of Nantes. It is
surrounded by a fine
park and has a swim-
ming pool. At least 20
rooms, starting at about
FF 650. The cuisine in
the restaurant is good.
Menus start at about
FF 275 (less expensive
weekly lunch menu).

Hôtel de la Côte
Champtoceaux
☎ 40.83.50.39
Sympathic, rural hotel
with almost 30 rooms
starting at about FF 150.
It is also a restaurant.

Don Quichotte
Vallet
☎ 40.33.99.67
Modern hotel surroun-
ding an old windmill and
near a roundabout. A
dozen rather small, yet
comfortable rooms,
starting at about FF 250.
Much seafood in the
restaurant, often
including oysters 'au
Muscadet'. One of the
best menus is around
FF 200.

Château de Cléray in Saint-Fiacre.

MUSCADET

It was the Romans, and later the monks, who
first practised viniculture around Nantes.
Originally, mainly black grapes grew in the
region but this began to change in the 17th
century. Thanks to the Dutch, a demand arose
for light, white wines for distillation, with the
result that more and more farmers began to grow
white grapes. The changeover from red to white
was forced in a dramatic way when, in 1709, all
the grapevines froze. The winter that year was so
severe that even the seawater of the nearby ocean
turned to ice. Of the white grapes that were then
planted, one finally dominated the rest: the
melon musqué de Bourgogne, later called
muscadet. The wine and the area of origin also
took this name. Muscadet is shaped like a broad
fan to the south and east of Nantes. The region
consists of three districts: Muscadet, Muscadet

RECOMMENDED PRODUCERS
All of these winegrowers and wine
dealers make a Muscadet 'sur lie',
sometimes even in several versions. The
best and most expensive wines are
always those from old grapevines; they
give wines with more aroma, taste and
concentration than the ordinary types of

Muscadet. Of the enormous number of
producers in Muscadet (about 3,000
vineyard owners plus about 40 wine
merchants) the following names form an
extremely modest selection. The estates
are almost always situated outside the
actual village centre. In most areas signs
point the way. Almost all of the

des Coteaux de la Loire and Muscadet de Sèvre et Maine. The latter is by far the largest and it contains 85 per cent of all the vineyards. In general, it also gives the best wines. A good Muscadet de Sèvre et Maine has a clear, light taste that is fresh without being sour. The types that are bottled 'sur lie', that is to say, straight from the tank in which the fermentation takes place, are more lively and fresher than the others. Because they are not pumped over to another, clean tank (without 'lie', the fermentation sediment) contact with oxygen often results in a slight effervescence. Apart from Muscadet, a second white wine is also produced in the region, Gros Plant du Pays Nantais. It tastes somewhat coarser and often has a high degree of acidity; the best types are also bottled 'sur lie'. The vineyards of the district of Sèvre et Maine are situated in and around the valleys of the Sèvre Nantaise and the Maine. The landscape is peaceful and consists of low hills alternating with flat plateaus. A pleasurable way to explore this district is to take the N 249 from Nantes in a southerly direction. Once over the Loire, if you so desire, you can turn off near *Basse-Goulaine*, from where a good road runs along the bank of the Loire in a northeasterly

Hôtel de la Gare
Clisson
℃ 40.36.16.55
About 35 rooms with prices up to about FF 300. Also a bar, restaurant and domestic catering firm. At walking distance from the covered market and the castle.
La Lande Saint-Martin
Haute-Goulaine
℃ 40.06.20.06
Well-equipped hotel

Old wine barn in Maisdon-sur-Sèvre.

municipalities mentioned are found in the district of Muscadet de Sèvre et Maine, where the recommended wine route is set out.
LA CHAPELLE BASSE-MER
Château la Berrière
Domaine de la Saulzaie
LA CHAPELLE-HEULIN

Donatien Bahuaud This firm owns Château de la Cassemichère (note the commemorative stone for the first planting of muscadet) and annually brings a superior Muscadet on to the market under the name of Master de Donatien.
Château des Gautronnières
Domaine de l'Hyvernière

along the N 149 with 40 rooms. Prices start at about FF 180 to FF 380. At the weekends it is often used for banquets and parties. You can eat very well in the restaurant. Expect to pay about FF 175 for a menu (but it is possible to pay less).

Les Voyageurs
Champtoceaux
℃ 40.83.50.09
Situated high above the Loire (good view) with 17 simple rooms starting at about FF 150. In the restaurant you can eat well (many fish dishes) and inexpensively.

RESTAURANTS
La Bonne Auberge
Clisson
℃ 40.54.01.90
The cuisine is excellent in this establishment on

direction. You could also drive on until a turn-off to *Haute-Goulaine*. The most impressive castle of Muscadet is found there, the Château de Goulaine. It was constructed at the end of the 15th century upon the ruins of a 10th-century fortress and, except for an interval of seven decades, has been in the hands of the same family for about a thousand years. Visitors may not only view the richly decorated salons, but also a volière in which some 200 butterflies flutter freely. Another place of interest in Haute-Goulaine is the more westerly situated chapel of Saint-Martin (18th-century). The journey continues by way of the D 105 to *Vertou*, a small city with a long history. In the churchyard there are sarcophagi from the Merovingian period and, from an abbey founded in the 11th century, there remains a 17th-century vestibule. At that time the monks made the Sèvre navigable; nowadays, in summer, you can take a boat trip along this river. Around Vertou there are windmills and the municipality maintains an aquarium at Beautour. By following the D 59 in a southerly direction, you pass the point where the Sèvre and the Maine flow into each other. Not long afterwards you will arrive in *Saint-Fiacre*, which is dominated by its curious Byzantine clock tower. Another tower, from the 15th century, is situated on the wine estate of Château de Chasseloir. The appellation Muscadet de Sèvre et

In the district of Sèvre et Maine.

Domaine de la Levraudière
CLISSON
Domaine de l'Epinay/Albert Paquereau
LA HAIE-FOUASSIERE
Le Fief du Breil
Domaine de la Louveterie
Daniel et Gérard Vinet

Haute-Goulaine
Château de Goulaine At present the marquis of Goulaine is making attractive wines, Muscadets as well as Gros Plant du Pays Nantais.
LE LANDREAU
Domaine de la Blanchetière
Château de Briacé

Le Pallet has a wine museum.

Maine originated in Saint-Fiacre and it is also said that the winegrowing land in this district is the most expensive of the entire region.

It is not a long drive to *La Haie-Fouassière*, on the north bank of the Sèvre. On the way, in *La Métairie*, a municipal bread oven can be seen. In La Haie-Fouassière the biscuits marketed under the French brand name LU are made and just outside the village stands the Maison des Vins de Nantes, where all possible wine information can be found. In a southwesterly direction is the Site des Cavernes, a viewing point near the Sèvre with a number of prehistoric caves. Now drive straight on, in a northerly direction, to *La Chapelle-Heulin*. From here, by way of the small canal

a square with a small, colourful garden. Fresh fish is always on the menu (sometimes prepared with a sabayon of oysters). Menus change daily and start at about FF 175 (less expensive weekly lunch menu). A fine wine list.

Le Cep de Vigne
La Haie-Fouassière
℃ 40.36.93.90
For about FF 100 you can enjoy a menu that is considerably more tasteful than the interior. Situated on the railway station square.

Domaine de l'Ecu
Domaine de la Grange
Domaine de la Momenière
Domaine de la Rocherie
Domaine de la Vrillonnière
LE LOUROUX-BOTTEREAU
Domaine de Hautes-Noëlles
MAISDON-SUR-SEVRE

Domaine de la Haute Févrie (in the hamlet of La Févrie)
Louis Métaireau et ses Vignerons d'Art Dynamic group of producers with a series of superior Muscadets. Maisdon is situated between Saint-Fiacre and Clisson.
MOUZILLON

Les Jardins de la Forge
Champtoceaux
© 40.83.56.23
One of the very best and most beautiful places to dine in the region. Perfectly furnished in spring-like tints and with an unusually refined cuisine of regional, as well as newly created, dishes. There is an excellent (weekly) menu for about FF 150. Situated next to the castle towers.

Mon Rêve
Basse-Goulaine
© 40.03.55.50
Dining in the garden here on a beautiful summer evening is quite an experience. Much emphasis is placed on fish, crustaceans and

port of Montru, wine vats were shipped down the Loire in the 19th century. The parish church dates from the 12th century and outside the village centre, on Château de la Cassemichère, stands a simple memorial stone which commemorates the fact that in May 1740 the first melon de Bourgogne was planted. (There are documents, however, which state that the same grape had already been introduced elsewhere in 1635.)

Southwards, small roads run to *Le Pallet*, a village on the N 149. Near the small River Sanguèze are the remains of a Roman road and a fort. The history of Le Pallet, local winegrowing and the lives of its two famous inhabitants are all celebrated in the Musée Pierre Abélard (a former chapel). Abélard was born in 1079 in a castle on the north side of the village (the ruins still exist). He is famous as a philosopher and for his tragic love affair with Heloïse. The second famous inhabitant is Admiral Roland Barin de la Galissonnière, who was governor of Quebec in the 18th century and also a botanist. Among other plants, he brought begonias and magnolias to Muscadet. From

Clisson with its Italian-looking church.

Philippe et Michel Chiron
Gérard et Michel Gaborit
Marcel-Joseph Guihoux
Guilbaud Frères Quality-oriented firm with its own land.
André Vinet
LE PALLET
Château de la Mercredière

Marcel Sautejeau Active wine dealer who produces a delicious Muscadet from his own Domaine de l'Hyvernière.
SAINT-FIACRE
Château de la Cantrie
Chéreau-Carré This firm supervises the distribution from a number of family properties, such as Domaine du Bois

Le Pallet you can follow two walking routes of 7 and 8 kilometres, respectively.

It is not a long drive to *Clisson*, the most striking municipality of the whole area. This small city is situated near the point where the Sèvre Nantaise and the Maine conjoin and its architecture is surprising because, in many cases, it is Italian. There are many houses with white walls and flat roofs with red tiles, while the 19th-century church of Notre-Dame could be from the middle of Italy. This Italian influence is the work of the brothers François (diplomat) and Pierre (painter) Cacault, who settled in the almost entirely ruined Clisson in

Château de Goulaine.

the year 1798, after a long stay in Italy. Together with the sculptor Frédéric Lemot, they bought the abandoned ruin of Clisson's castle – which had been built in the 13th century by Oliver I of Clisson, after his return from the crusades – and began to design first one and later more houses in the Italian-Romantic style. One of these was the Maison Garenne-Lemot, a villa built on the lines of a Tuscan model, which nowadays functions as an exhibition centre for modern art. The example of the Cacaults and Lemot was followed by others, so that more houses, and even factories, were built in the Italian style, as

shellfish, with or without beurre blanc or other sauces. Various menus, among them a very good one for about FF 220. The restaurant is situated on a dike by the Loire, on the east side of the village.

La Pierre Percée
La Chapelle Basse-Mer
✆ 40.06.33.09
For about FF 200 you can enjoy a tasty meal. One of the specialities is pike perch in beurre

Bruley, Château de Chasseloir, Château de Coing Saint-Fiacre and Grand Fief de la Cormeraie. The quality of the wines is high.
Domaine de Gras-Moutons
Domaine de la Hautière
Domaine de la Tourmaline
Saint-Géréon

Jacques Guindon In this village on the north bank of the Loire near Ancenis, a beautiful Muscadet des Coteaux is produced by the Guindon family.
Vallet
Domaine des Bégaudières
Domaine Chiron
Château du Cléray/Sauvion Fils Very

blanc. Save some Muscadet for the goat cheese.

Gallo-roman bridge in Mouzillon.

Restaurant de la Vallée
Clisson
✆ 40.54.36.23
This is situated next to one of the old bridges and offers a view of the castle and the church of Notre-Dame. Regional cuisine and wines. Menus start at about FF 110 (less expensive weekly lunch menu). When the weather is sunny you can eat on the terrace.

TOURIST TIPS
• In La Boissière-du-Doré, a village halfway between Clisson and Ancenis, there is a zoo.

well as the city hall and the previously mentioned church of Notre-Dame. The heart of the village also has large, wooden market halls from the 15th century. You can cross the Sèvre by means of two old bridges. The churches of La Trinité and St Jacques are partially Romanesque and in the churchyard (which is situated in the middle of the Henri IV park) there are the Temple de l'Amitié and the tombstones of, and memorials to the Cacaults and their friend Lemot.

From Clisson the D 763 runs to *Mouzillon*, a modest wine village with a large church and a small Gallic-Romanic bridge (south side, look for the sign). *Vallet* then comes into view, the 'capitale du Muscadet'. Many wine activities take place here. Vallet also has a gypsy graveyard. One of the most interesting castles of the neighbourhood is the Château La Noë which dates from 1936. The next point on our journey is Le Landreau, an important wine municipality that has a school of viticulture and a research centre. On the way to *Le Louroux-Bottereau* you will pass windmills (at Pé; also a viewing point). In front of the local church stands one of the few statues of Louis XVI and inside the church you can see two 12th-century frescos. By way of *La Chapelle Basse-Mer* and *La Varenne* (where we leave Sèvre et Maine for Muscadet des Coteaux de la Loire) the route continues to

energetic family firm, which not only makes wine in its own castle but also produces a series of marvellous Muscadets that are selected and bottled on other properties. They are offered under the name Les Découvertes, with brand names such as Lauréat and Cardinal Richard.

Drouet Frères
Domaine du Grand Verré
Château de la Guipière
Josep Hallereau
Domaine du Montys
Château la Noë Worth a visit just to see the building itself.
Château de la Ragotière

Champtoceaux. It is situated high above the Loire and offers a delightful panorama across the open countryside. In the village there is the ruin of a citadel flanked by two towers. In earlier times a toll was collected here. The Muscadet trip can be concluded by either crossing the Loire near Champtoceaux and going to Ancenis by way of the wine village *Saint-Géréon*, or by following the south bank and driving to Ancenis by way of *Liré*. Here, in a village on a hill, Joachim du Bellay was born in about 1525, in the 13th-century Château de la Turmelière (now a ruin). A museum devoted to this Renaissance poet is set up in a house dating from the 16th century.

Many estates are indicated.

- Every Friday evening there is a large livestock market in Clisson where a few thousand cattle are sold.
- Clisson organises a sound and light show, Les Tambours du Val de Sèvre, a few times in summer. In the same city guides are also available for walks among the monuments.

Château de la Touche
Domaine de la Tourlaudière
VERTOU
Domaine de la Borne

RELATED TO WINE
- Every year in March the largest wine fair of the region takes place here: the

Foire aux Vins in Vallet. It is generally held on the third weekend in March. A smaller wine exchange usually occurs two weeks earlier in Le Louroux-Bottereau, which usually stages its wine festival in October.
- There is a wine tasting room in the castle of Clisson.

HOTEL
Akwaba
Boulevard Dr. Moutel
℡ 40.83.30.30
This is the largest and
most modern local
hotel, with about 50
rooms starting at about
FF 270. It also has a
restaurant.

COTEAUX D'ANCENIS

The wine area of Coteaux d'Ancenis lies within
the borders of Muscadet des Coteaux de la Loire
(see the previous chapter). Red and rosé wines
are mainly produced, usually from the gamay,
but there are also nice red wines from the
cabernet franc, and white from the chenin blanc
and malvoisie (pinot gris). Most of them taste
fresh and pleasing without being really
memorable. The heart of this modest wine area is
the city of Ancenis on the north bank of the
Loire. A castle, the entrance of which is marked
by two 15th-century towers, stands near the 500-
metre-long suspension bridge that spans this

The castle of Ancenis, where Brittany and France concluded their treaty.

RECOMMENDED PRODUCERS
Domaine des Genaudières (Le Cellier)
This is one of the largest individual
producers of Coteaux d'Ancenis, with a
complete range of red, rosé and white
wines (also Muscadets and Gros Plant).
**Domaine des Grandes Pierres
Meslières** (Saint-Géréon) Rather sturdy

red wines and a fruity Gamay rosé.
Jacques Guindon (Saint-Géréon)
Excells with its Muscadet des Coteaux de
la Loire and also with rosé and red
Gamay, while the white Malvoisie usually
has a slighly sweet taste.
Domaine l'Ouche Guinière (Saint-
Géréon) Reliable wine estate for rosé

river. The fortress was built between the 14th and 16th centuries and it was here, in 1468, that Duke Francis I of Brittany and Louis XI of France signed the treaty that prepared for Brittany's entry into the French empire. The castle can be visited; you will see various architectural styles, such as that of the Renaissance in the largest pavilion. In the park near the castle there is a large cedar tree and a statue of the poet Joachim du Bellay (to whom the Muscadet village of Liré has devoted a museum). Behind the castle is the old city centre, with narrow streets, a restored market hall from the time of Napoleon III and a spacious square with the church of Saint-Pierre-et-Saint-Paul (15th/16th century). From the river quay at Ancenis much wine was shipped in the early 1800s. At that time many coopers were active in the city, commemorated in street names such as rue des Tonneliers. In the same period many sails for inland shipping were produced locally. Nowadays neither wine nor ships play an important role and it will cost the visitor some effort to find any trace of them. By far the largest wine producer is a gigantic food co-operative along the road to Angers. Next to the entrance an almost-hidden dolmen can be found. This grave monument dates from Gallic times and proves that Ancenis has an extremely long history.

RESTAURANT
Auberge Bel Air
℘ 40.83.02.87
Situated along the n 23, in the direction of Angers (on a sloping bend in the road). In good weather you can eat on the terrace. Menus start at about FF 115. There is a stylish interior. Much fish and seafood, such as *St Jacques du pays à la nage du Muscadet*. A good view over the Loire.

and, above all, red from the gamay.
Les Vignerons de la Noëlle (Ancenis) This co-operative produces more Coteaux d'Ancenis than all the other producers together. The quality is good because the wines are professionally prepared. One of the most pleasing wines from the collection is the red Gamay which has a

strong fruity taste. Wines from the Muscadet, Anjou and Touraine are also available.

ANJOU

In Anjou (named after a former province) the wine grape has been grown since about the 3rd century. Nowadays this region produces about a quarter of all the Loire wines and it is striking how large the variety is. White wines, which can be dry, semi-dry or sweet, different sorts of rosé, a large amount of sparkling wine and various types of red wine are made here. In total, Anjou has about 25 different appellations. Despite the prominent production of wine, the area also produces many other things, including cherries and flowers, while much coal was formerly mined, often even in the middle of the wine area. Anjou mainly comprises the department of Maine et Loire, with parts of Deux Sèvre and Vienne. The average annual temperature is one degree higher than that of Paris and relatively little rain fall – about 600 millimetres a year. The landscape is often very lovely. Vineyards, fields and meadows alternate with orchards, woods and nurseries. The terrain has an undulating relief almost everywhere, which gives marvellous, and constantly changing, panoramic views. Above all, in and around the valley of the Layon, beautiful views can be enjoyed, especially on sunny autumn days when the wine slopes are clothed in a glowing habit of brown-gold tints. Elsewhere in the region, particularly around Saumur, you will find many caves carved out of tufa stone. These are former quarries, which nowadays are used for the storage of wine or the cultivation of mushrooms. In earlier times people lived in the caves – and this sometimes still occurs. Another characteristic element of the landscape is its numerous windmills, estimated at about 650 in number. Most of them have a stone base and have now lost their vanes: they remind one of watchtowers. There are still some intact windmills, however, which can usually be visited. It is perhaps not by chance that much trade has taken place between the two peoples who made the building of windmills their speciality, the Dutch and the people of Anjou. In the 16th and 17th centuries the Dutch promoted the production of sweet white wines in Anjou. Dutch agents often bought entire harvests and had them shipped in Dutch vessels to Dutch ports. In 1681 the mayor of Rotterdam declared that the wine trade with Anjou was of vital importance to his city. Dutch influence disappeared as a result of war and the French Revolution but many sweet white wines can still be found in Anjou.

ANGERS

The capital of Anjou and of the department of Sèvre et Maine is situated not on the Loire but on the Maine, a river that is only about 10 kilometres long. The history of Angers goes back to the Gallic period, but its most striking monument dates from a later time: the

Rose window of the Saint-Maurice cathedral.

castle on the Maine quay. Commissioned by Louis IX (Saint Louis), it arose in about 1240 on the site of a wooden fort and stands on a rock about 30 metres in height. Around the bulwark lies a moat, in which water from the Maine once flowed but which nowadays serves as a garden. The almost 1,000-metre-long wall is emphasised by 17 powerful, half-round towers, some 40 to 50 metres in height. The building materials used were a pale sandstone and a dark slate which was often used elsewhere in Angers. Within the ramparts there is a large courtyard with a chapel, the modest lodgings of Le Bon Roi René, the Logis Royal of Louis II and a garden in the French style. In the Logis Royal and other buildings a wonderful collection of tapestries is displayed. The most famous series is the Apocalypse, which was made in the second half of the 14th century and was commissioned by Louis I, Duke of Anjou. At a length of 100 metres, it is France's longest gobelin; it was worked on for seven years and comprises 70 tapestries. Elsewhere in Angers other tapestries can also be admired, as in the cathedral of Saint-Maurice, not far from the castle. To a large part the building dates from the 12th and 13th centuries, although some sections were added later, including the central tower. The nave is unusually broad and has marvellous stained glass windows from the 12th and 15th centuries. The best-known tapestry here is the Stoning of Saint-Etienne. On the opposite bank of the Maine, next to each other, are two museums in which tapestries also feature. The Musée

Jean Lurçat bears the name of a painter who, in 1938, was so inspired
by the Apocalypse that he made his own version of it, also in the form
of gobelins. Lurçat (who died in 1966) called his series Chant du
Monde. The tapestries are exhibited in the large hall of the former
13th-century hospital of Saint-Jean. Nine years' work went into the
series by Lurçat, which is in strong visual contrast to the other
Apocalypse. Next to the hospital museum is the Musée de la Tapisserie
Contemporaine, where artists from the second half of the present
century show their work.

Along the slightly sloping rue Toussaint, between the castle and the
cathedral, is the entrance to the Galerie David d'Angers. It is situated
in the church of a former abbey; the building has been strikingly
restored with a glass roof. David d'Angers (1788-1856) was a gifted
sculptor, much of whose work can be seen here. Around the corner of
the rue Toussaint is the Logis Barrault, where the Musée des Beaux-
Arts is situated. It has a considerable collection of paintings, which
includes canvases by Boucher, Philippe de Champaigne, Chardin,
Corot, Maurice Denis, Fragonard, Ingres and Watteau. While mostly
French works can be seen in the Logis Barrault, the Musée Pincé
exhibits art from other civilisations, including Greek, Roman,
Egyptian, Chinese and Japanese. The latter museum is situated in the
rue Lenepveu, a pedestrian precinct not far from the place du
Ralliement, the heart of the downtown area. The square is surrounded
by splendid buildings, among which is the theatre. By walking from
the square in the direction of the Maine, you come to the place de la
République, where a contemporary shopping mall has been built. For
those who wish to discover the wines and vineyards of Anjou, it will be
worthwhile to pay a short visit to the Maison du Vin de l'Anjou, on
the place Kennedy, near the entrance to the castle. Information about
Angers and its surroundings is given by the Office du Tourisme on the
same square. Also worth a visit is the Château de Pignerolle, a
museum situated on the east side of Angers, in the suburb of Saint-
Barthélémy. The exhibition here takes as its theme 'from the tom-tom
to the satellite' and is devoted to a study of human communication.

Grape picking in Coteaux du Layon.

HOTELS
Le Castel
Brissac-Quincé
☎ 41.91.24.74
Situated in the heart of
the village, within
walking distance of the
castle. A dozen,
pleasant rooms starting
at about FF 200. Friendly
service. No restaurant.

THE VINEYARDS OF ANJOU

No Loire area produces such divergent wines as
Anjou. Here you wil find dry, semi-dry and sweet
white wines, sparkling wines, dry and semi-dry
rosés and many sorts of red wine. It is striking
that most of the winegrowers produce an almost
complete range. Whoever visits the Anjou cellars
wil, in most cases, be offered ten or more
different wines to taste. This is the first reason
why time is necessary on a trip through Anjou.
The second is that Anjou stretches over a large
area in which there is much to see. Thus, if you
follow the route described, you must reckon on
at least a day or two – especially if you intend to

RECOMMENDED PRODUCERS
BEAULIEU-SUR-LAYON
Château du Breuil Situated in the
hamlet of the same name, which is built
on a hill with a panoramic view across the
Layon valley. In the well-preserved, 19th-
century castle, they produce, among
others, a fine Coteaux du Layon Beaulieu

from old vines and a fleshy Anjou Villages.
Château Pierre Bise This wine estate,
which is dynamically run by Claude Papin,
takes its name from the hamlet of Pierre
Bise and covers about 40 hectares in
various appellations. The average quality
of the wines is high, as is shown by,
among others, the white Anjou Sec, the

stop often to take a walk, taste wine and visit museums or monuments. The route is limited to the wine districts on the south bank of the Loire. A separate chapter is devoted to the small area of Savennières on the

Rochefort-sur-Loire has a sixteenth century church tower.

north bank. We begin in Montjean-sur-Loire, about 25 kilometres from Ancenis, but the trip can also be made from Angers in reverse order. That *Montjean-sur-Loire*, a village built partially against a slope, has had a prosperous past is shown by its enormous church. In the 18th and 19th centuries the village lived from coal and lime and it was also a centre for inland shipping. In and around Montjean there were 14 lime kilns, set on constructions that looked like towers. The past is brought to life in the local Ecomusée, which has been established in a former smithy. From the museum, visits to the lime kilns, coal mines and vineyards are organised, while various boat trips are also possible. Then, by way of the D 15, you travel on to *La Pommeraye*, a wine village that belongs to the appellation Anjou Coteaux de la Loire. This is a rather rare, generally semi-sweet white wine. Its grape is the chenin blanc (also called pineau

Château des Chateliers
Murs-Erigné
℗ 41.45.90.00
Comfortable place to stay near the Loire, on the west side of the village. Prices start at about FF 450. Two restaurants: a grill and the gastronomic *Le Chevreuil* (menus start at about FF 180). There is also a tearoom.

Hôtel de France
Doué-la-Fontaine
℗ 41.59.12.27
About 20 simple rooms starting at about FF 150. In the restaurant you can enjoy a tasty meal for less than FF 100.

exemplary Anjou Village, which is wood-ripened and supplied with berry-like fruit, the Coteaux du Layon Beaulieu, the Quarts de Chaume and the Savennières Clos de Coulaine, of which Papin has leased the vineyard since 1992.
Domaine de la Soucherie Superlative Coteaux du Layon Chaume and various

other good wines, including Savennières. The estate was bought from the marquis of Brissac in 1952.
BONNEZEAUX
Château de Fesles Property of the famous Parisian pâtissier Gaston Lenôtre, who has invested heavily in the castle as well as the cellars. He is the most

Grand Hôtel
Rochefort-sur-Loire
℗ 41.78.80.46
This small business,
which has eight rooms,
was partially restored in
1992. Rather thin-
walled. Always try to
get a room at the rear.
Prices start at about
FF 200. Delicious meals
for less than FF 100. Ask
for the *salade paysanne*.

de la Loire), which is also used in the other white Loire wines. This is usually the only variety used; only in Anjou Sec is it now often complemented with the Bourgogne grape chardonnay (up to a maximum of 20 per cent), this dry wine thereby acquiring somewhat more fruit and dimension. From La Pommeraye – which has an old watermill, Moulin de Bêne – the journey continues on the D 15 and D 751 to *Chalonnes-sur-Loire*. This is one of the oldest villages in Anjou.

The Domaine des Baumard in Rochefort-sur-Loire.

Near the bank of the Loire is the church of Saint-Maurille (the choir dates from the 12th century) and, in the centre, the Notre-Dame de Chalonnes (the oldest section is 12th-century). A 15th-century tower remains from an episcopal palace. The Musée la Brairie is devoted to the production of hemp, which was formerly very important in this part of Anjou. Chalonnes was also one of the villages where the Dutch bought much wine in the 17th century in order to ship it back home. The 'vins pour la mer' were always of better quality than the 'vins pour Paris', which remained in France. In the summer, Chalonnes has a popular tourist

important producer of Bonnezeaux wine, and also a trend-setting one. Several other wines are made as well: red and Chardonnay (Vin de Pays).

BOUILLÉ-LORETZ

Domaine de la Gretonnelle In this most southerly municipality of Anjou (situated in Deux Sèvres), a wide range of

good wines is produced by this estate.

BRISSAC QUINCÉ

Domaine de Bablut A large range of modern vinified wines, including Coteaux de l'Aubance. It also works with the label Château de Brissac.

Les Caves de la Loire Large co-operative.

attraction in the form of a train which runs through the vineyards. Chalonnes does not only fall within the regional appellation of Anjou and Coteaux de l'Aubance, but

Windmill at Faye d'Anjou.

also within that of Coteaux du Layon. This is named after the small River Layon, along the banks of which wine has been made since at least the 4th century. Coteaux du Layon is a pure chenin wine, made from overripe grapes, preferably affected by 'noble rot'. This causes the grapes to dry out, by which means they gain in sweetness and the pulp acquires a special aroma. Because *pourriture noble* doesn't affect all the grapes at the same time, the farmers make their pickers go through the vineyards several times. Coteaux du Layon forms an elegant combination of sweet fruits, honey, nuts and spices; drinking it has been described by the French gourmet Curnonsky as 'a walk with a ravishing blonde under blooming lime trees under a beautiful Sunset'. On the labels of the best Coteaux du Layon you will usually find the name of a village such as Beaulieu or Chaume.
Chaudefonds-sur-Layon is the next stop. The

RESTAURANTS
Le Clémenceau
Brissac-Quincé
✆ 41.91.22.01
Near the *Le Castel* hotel. Various menus (with, among others, pike perch and chicken) for under FF 100 and a very inexpensive daily menu (often *pot-au-feu*).

Domaine de Sainte Anne Striking Cabernet d'Anjou and a successful Anjou Villages and Coteaux de l'Aubance.
CHAUDEFONDS-SUR-LAYON
Domaine des Hauts-Perrays For Coteaux du Layon.
Domaine Gaudard Large range of wines.
CHAVAGNES-LES-EAUX

Domaine du Petit Val One of the better producers of Bonnezeaux, although they also make other good wines. The Goizil family displays a small collection of old tools and the precursor of the modern bicycle in the tasting cellar.
CONCOURSON-SUR-LAYON
Château des Rochettes Some of the

Les Relais de Bonnezeaux
Bonnezeaux
© 41.54.08.33
Situated in the former station of Thouarcé-Bonnezeaux, which is on a hill. You dine in a sort of conservatory with a lot of glass. Very good cuisine, in which the wine of Bonnezeaux is often used. Inexpensive lunch menu on weekdays. Normal menus start at about FF 100.

name comes from Calidus Fons, which means 'warm fountain'. There is a spring here whose water is always around 15 degrees Celsius. A covered bathing place (17th-century) was built here. The village also has a large lime kiln and a medieval span bridge. By first taking the D 121 and then the D 17, we arrive in *Saint-Lambert-du-Lattay*. From April to the end of October, the Musée de la Vigne et du Vin d'Anjou can be visited. It has five rooms in which aspects of wine culture are displayed. In the village you can take a small walk through the vineyards (with or without a guide). Now take the D 125 to *Saint-Aubin-de-Luigné*. In this 'jewel of the Layon' the city hall has been housed in a fine, 16th-century parsonage. Elsewhere in the village there are

Domaine de la Soucherie in Beaulieu-sur-Layon.

cellars are situated in a former stable. Beautiful Coteaux du Layon.
DOUÉ-LA-FONTAINE
Touchais Wine merchant who also owns a lot of vineyards and produces a fantastic Coteaux du Layon, Moulin Touchais.
FAYE D'ANJOU

Domaine de Haut Mont A Bonnezeaux from old vines, which is full of character, and a stylish Coteaux du Layon Faye.
Leblanc et Fils Owners of the Moulin de la Pinsonnerie (fine panorama). Bonnezeaux, Coteaux du Layon, Anjous.
MARTIGNÉ-BRIAND
Domaine de Brizé Attractive wines

various buildings from the same period. You can go on walking trips or rent a boat in order to cross the Layon (only in the summer). Now drive to *La Haie-Longue* (good view) and then across the *corniche angevine* to *Rochefort-sur-Loire*. The clock tower of the large church of Sainte-Croix is 16th-century and various houses date from the period between the 15th and 17th centuries. From Rochefort we go inland once again, first a little way along the D 54 and then, near a fork, right to the hamlet of *Chaume*. This is the place of origin of Coteaux du Layon Chaume as well as Quarts de Chaume. The latter, very small appellation is thus named because in former times the lord of the manor had the right to one-quarter of the wine harvest and usually took the best – the wines from Chaume. A good Quarts de Chaume is still richer than a Coteaux du Layon. This has to do with the somewhat warmer microclimate. In common with Coteaux du Layon, this wine can ripen for decades. From Chaume we drive back in a northerly direction and, at the D 55, turn right. After passing the wine hamlets of *Le Breuil* and *La Pierre Bise*, *Beaulieu-sur-Layon* comes into sight. Here there is a Romanesque chapel with 12th-century

Old dovecote, Château de la Guimonière.

Restaurant Vigneron
Saint-Aubin-de-Luigné
℃ 41.78.33.15
Charming place to eat where, for very little money, you can enjoy fresh fish with *beurre blanc* – the speciality. It is situated on the church square.

(such as Anjou Villages, Coteaux du Layon and a Crémant de Loire.
MOZÉ-SUR-LOUET
Domaine Richou Producer of award-winning wines. Anjou Sec Chauvigné, three red Anjous, Coteaux de l'Aubance and Chardonnay (Vin de Pays).
Domaine des Rochettes A varied range of wines with a good balance between price and quality. Wines such as Coteaux de l'Aubance, Anjou Villages, various rosés and Chardonnay (Vin de Pays).
PASSAVANT-SUR-LAYON
Château de Passavant Excellent Anjou Villages, dry, white Anjou, and Coteaux du Layon.

The different styles of the Château de Brissac.

frescos, as well as a 19th-century church with a beautiful pulpit. Near the village you can also find a dolmen, a large forest and, on the west side, a viewing point. Now take the road to *Rablay-sur-Layon*, which you will see from the vantage point of a wine slope, lying in a hollow. Near a road junction in the village there is a 15th-century, half-timbered house, nowadays a post office. In the spring and summer, art exhibitions are organised in Rablay. A retable dating from the 18th century can be admired in the church. Now take the D 125 in the direction of Thouarcé, turn off to *La Touche* and drive through to *Faye d'Anjou*. Along the way signposts will direct you to the Moulin de la Pissonnerie (panorama and

LA POMMERAYE
Domaine du Fresche One of the better producers of semi-sweet Coteaux de la Loire. The Anjou Sec (with chardonnay) is also worth discovering.
ROCHEFORT-SUR-LOIRE
Domaine des Baumard The congenial Jean Baumard and his son Florent number among the very best wine producers of the region. In their 17th-century building they make, among others, an exemplary Quarts de Chaume, as well as various sorts of Coteaux du Layon and sublime wines from Savennières, including a Clos du Papillon which is always very aromatic.

Stone quarries, Doué-la-Fontaine.

wine estate). In Anjou there are many windmills, some complete, others with only their stone bases left. These windmills are called 'caviers'. Some date from the late 14th century. From Faye, drive on to *Bonnezeaux*, a hamlet belonging to the municipality of Thouarcé, which, like Quarts de Chaume, produces a gracious, sweet, white wine of longevity with its own appellation. In *Thouarcé* the fortified Manoir de Chanzé (15th-century) stands near the Layon. The local church is 12th-century. The next stop is at *Chavagnes-les-Eaux*, where there are excavations dating from the Roman period. Then travel on to *Martigné-Briand*, also called the 'capital of the Cabernet

- Flowers and wine are combined during a festival in Martigné-Briand on the first weekend in August.
- In Dénézé-sous-Doué (along the d 69, north of Doué-la-Fontaine), more than 300 sculptures of human figures have been found in a cave – among them an American Indian. The work dates from the 16th century.

Bonnezeaux's largest producer is the Château de Fesles.

Château de Belle Rive Situated near the hamlet of Chaume, this is the largest producer of Quarts de Chaume. Elegant, sweet wine with the subtle, slight bitterness of quince; it can keep for a very long time.

Château de Bellevue Admirable Coteaux du Layon Chaume, followed closely by the just as priceless Coteaux du Layon Rochefort and various dry Anjous in white and red.

Domaine Grosset-Château Several old vintages are available of the Coteaux du Layon Rochefort. The 1986 was a relatively recent success.

Château de la Guimonière A 16thd'Anjou'. This is a semi-sweet rosé from the cabernet franc. Ordinary Rosé d'Anjou is usually made from the groslot (or grolleau). Dry rosé also exists: Rosé de Loire (with at least 30 per cent cabernet). Because the demand for rosé is falling, many winegrowers from Anjou have

The town hall of Saint-Aubin-de-Luigné is an old parsonage.

applied themselves to red wines, such as Anjou Gamay (also as a primeur), red Anjou from cabernet or a mix of grapes, and Anjou Villages. The latter is always the best. Its appellation consists of no less than 50 municipalities and the cabernet sauvignon and/or cabernet franc are the prescribed grapes. The wine is also often ripened in wood. Martigné-Briand can be recognised from a distance by the high spire of the church of Saint-Simplicin, as well as by the sturdy remains of a 16th-century castle. In the castle cellar (12th-15th-century) wine can be tasted. The road goes on to *Aubigné-sur-Layon* which has a Romanesque church and the remains of a castle from the 15th and 16th centuries. Then by way of the D 748 and D 48, we go on to the attractive village of *Tigné* (watch for the signs), where film star Gérard Depardieu owns the Château de Tigné and also makes wine. If you have the time, you could now travel on

century castle with delicious wines.
Domaine de ia Motte This is situated along the road that runs through Rochefort (east side) and produces a superior Coteaux du Layon Rochefort, as well as an ample series of other wines.
Château de Piëgüe Various wines that are just as charming as the view here,

such as the white Anjou Sec and Coteaux du Layon Rochefort. Around the 19th-century castle grow hundreds of parasol pines.
Domaine de la Pierre-Sainte-Maurille Recommended for its red Anjou and Coteaux du Layon Saint-Aubin. Beautiful view.

The hamlet of Chaume, the cradle of Coteaux du Layon Chaume.

narrow roads in a southerly direction to *Passavant-sur-Layon* in order to see the remains of a castle (where wine can be tasted), as well as the Romanesque apse in the church. Still further south, in the department of Deux Sèvres, is *Bouillé-Loretz*, a village with several old buildings and the ruins of the abbey of Serrière. From Tigné you can actually drive direct to Doué-la-Fontaine, with or without a digression to *Concourson-sur-Layon*, where the church of Saint-Hilaire dates from the 11th century. In the south of Anjou is *Doué-la-Fontaine*, which, with about 7,300 inhabitants, is the largest city. On the side of Concourson there is a nice zoo. Not far from here (follow the signs) is

Château de Plaisance It is pleasant to stay here, not only because of the view but also because of the wines.
SAINT-AUBIN-DE-LUIGNÉ
Domaine des Forges Many different sorts of wines, varying from a crowned Anjou Gamay Primeur and Anjou Villages, solely from cabernet, to sweet Coteaux du Layon from Chaume and Saint-Aubin.
Château de la Roulerie The best wine is the Coteaux du Layon Chaume, but the Anjou Sec with chardonnay also has merit.
SAINT-JEAN-DES-MAUVRETS
Château d'Avrillé Extended estate, expertly worked.

the Château du Baron Foullon, an historic monument dating from the 17th century. Near the castle a fine rose garden has been laid out. You will also find the Musée des Commerces Anciens here, devoted mainly to vanished professions. Not far from Doué's centre there are stone quarries (Les Perrières) in which dwellings have been carved. They can be visited by appointment. That the history of Doué-la-Fontaine dates back to the Roman time is proved by Les Arènes, a small Gallic-Romanic arena with a few cave cellars. Doué-la-Fontaine could be a starting point for a trip to Montreuil-Bellay

'Noble rot' in Coteaux du Layon.

or Saumur (see the chapter on Saumur) but the Anjou route continues in a northerly direction along the D 761, after which the turn-off to *Rochemenier* is taken. This hamlet consists of two parts, of which the largest is found underground, being formed by cave dwellings and farms, plus a chapel. In the part that can be visited two wine presses are on display.

Back on the D 761 your journey continues to Saulgé-l'Hôpital, where you turn off to *Grézillé*. There are cave dwellings here, while to the south stands the 15th-century Château de Pimpéan. Just before Grézillé, the small Aubance river is crossed,

Jean-Yves et Hubert Lebreton Serious wine makers offering, among others, a firm Anjou Villages and Coteaux de l'Aubance.

SAINT-LAMBERT-DU-LATTAY

Domaine des Bohues Pure Coteaux du Layon.

Domaine des Maurières Of the ten or

so wines that the Moron family make, the Coteaux du Layon Sélection Rive Gauche and the Quarts de Chaume stand out.

Domaine Ogereau Situated near the local wine museum. Eminent Coteaux du Layon Saint-Lambert.

SAINTE-MELANIE-SUR-AUBANCE

Domaine de Haute-Perche This wine

which has given its name to Coteaux de l'Aubance, a district that produces a modest amount of semi-sweet wines, usually somewhat fresher than those from Coteaux du Layon. By way of Chemellier we now drive to *Coutures*. In

Castle tower in Martigné-Briand

estate (owner Christian Papin) has a tasting room on the D 48 from Brissac to Angers. With the help of modern techniques, various good wines.

THOUARCÉ

Domaine de la Petite Croix A few types of Bonnezeaux.

Domaine de Terrebrune A wine estate founded by three winegrowers, which produces an absolutely superior Bonnezeaux. Old wine presses can be seen in the tasting room.

TIGNÉ

Château de Tigné This partially 11th-century castle is the property of film star Gérard Depardieu. This is why the tasting

the environs of this village there are many windmills and you will also find a dolmen here. Apart from wine, artichokes are an important local product; Coutures mounts an annual artichoke market. Along the D 751 in a northwesterly direction, the next village is *Saint-Jean-des-Mauvrets*, where there are several houses dating from the 15th and 16th centuries. The D 232 runs to *Saint-Melanie-sur-Aubance*, which has an ancient little church dating from the 10th century. Now we go a few kilometres south to *Brissac-Quincé*. In a park here is one of France's tallest castles, the Château de Brissac. Some of the 150 rooms are richly furnished. In one of the rooms there hangs a painted portrait of the widow Clicquot, from the Champagne house of the same name. There is also a small theatre in the building, while, in a larger room, the competition of Anjou Villages takes place every year. The castle was rebuilt at various times from the 15th to the 17th centuries and, as a result, exhibits quite a few different architectural styles. Another place of interest is the 16th-century church with an underground chapel and marvellous stained-glass windows. Not far outside the village there is an old windmill. Now take the D 55 to *Vauchrétien*. The road runs steeply upwards to a large wine plateau. It is worthwhile to stop and look back because there is beautiful view of Brissac-Quincé and its surroundings. Vauchrétien is a wine village of Gallic-Romanic origins. In the restored church old wall paintings can be admired, while the

room exhibits mementos from the film career of the owner. In the wine range there is a wood-ripened Anjou Villages with the name Cuvée Cyrano.

VAUCHRÉTIEN

Domaine Dittière In this former fief of the castle of Brissac delicious wines, such as Coteaux de l'Aubance and red Anjou plus Anjou Villages, are made.

Domaine de la Douesnerie Of the ten or so wines, the Anjou Sec and Anjou Villages deserve your attention.

Château la Varière Dry, white Anjou, various sorts of Coteaux du Layon and an Anjou Villages from cabernet.

In Coteaux du Layon the winegrowers like to sell to passers-by.

wood carving is worth a visit. The last village on our expedition through the vineyards of Anjou is *Mozé-sur-Louet*. This has a nice town hall and an ancient windmill, Moulin de la Bigottière. If you wish, the journey can be continued into Savennières (by crossing the river near Rochefort-sur-Loire), into Angers or to the area of Saumur.

RELATED TO WINE

- Last weekend of February: wine fair in Chalonnes-sur-Loire.
- Easter Monday: wine festival in Rablay-sur-Layon.
- First weekend in June: the Fête des Vins Rosés in Tigné.
- The Sunday before 14 July: the Fête de la Vinée in Saint-Lambert-du-Lattay.
- The Sunday after 14 July: wine festival in Saint-Aubin-de-Luigné.
- The first weekend in September: the Fête du Bonnezeaux in Thouarcé.
- The last weekend in November: harvest festival in Bouillé-Loretz.

♀ **HOTEL**
⌇ **L'Ancre du Marine**
Bouchemaine-La Pointe
🕾 41.77.14.46
Seasonal business with
a dozen rooms (starting
at about FF 175). Most
of the guests come here
for the restaurant,
where fish menus are
mainly served, starting
at about FF 100. It can
be reached most easily
by way of Savennières
and Epiré.

SAVENNIÈRES

Striking, generally dry, white wines are the
hallmark of Savennières, a tiny district west of
Angers. It takes its name from the village of
Savennières, which is ancient in origin and was
once called Vicus Saponaria, the Place of Soap,
because the water here was, apparently, very
aromatic. One of the oldest churches in Anjou is
found in Savennières: the oldest part is said to
date from the 9th or 10th century. The clock
tower is 12th-century and a room was added on
in the 15th century. Inside you will find the
remains of wall paintings. From Savennières a
narrow road goes to the hamlet of Epiré. First,
you follow a canal and a railway line; directly
thereafter the road winds upwards. Some parts of
this 75-hectare district are so steep that they
cannot be worked mechanically. Monks planted
the first grapevines here, and Savennières was

later drunk at the
court of Louis XIV
as well as by
Napoleon. Within
the appellation
Savennières there
are two
subdistricts:
Savennières
Coulée de Serrant
(7 hectares, one
owner) and
Savennières La

In Epiré a church functions as a wine cellar.

🛢 **RECOMMENDED PRODUCERS**
Clos de Coulaine (Savennières) Since
1992 it has been run by Claude Papin from
the Château Pierre Bise (see the previous
chapter). Small production, good wine
which demands time.
Domaine du Closel (Savennières)
Aromatic, elegant wine often with a

beautiful tint. Lovely castle.
Domaine des Baumard (Rochefort-sur-
Loire) See the previous chapter.
Château de Chamboureau
(Savennières) The Soulez brothers make
many kinds of Savennières, which are all
of high quality. The star of the range is
Château de Chamboureau Savennières

Roche-aux-Moines, four times as large. Previously, the wine tended to taste semi-sweet to sweet, but nowadays it is generally mineral-dry. Some producers make wine that only acquires charm after a number of years, while others make a supple wine for immediate consumption, which is very fragrant, with soft fruit plus a hint of spices in its aroma. Throughout Savennières and Epiré about 15 winegrowers are active, some of whom do not live here but on the south bank. Diminutive Epiré has two churches: a normal

Clos de la Coulée de Serrant.

one (with a map) and, on an attractive little square nearby, a much smaller and older church (11th-century), which has served for years as the wine cellar of Château d'Epiré. You can reach the district by way of Angers but it is much easier and more peaceful to cross the river near Rochefort-sur-Loire. This road runs across

Savennières and its church.

the charming Ile de Béhuard, a famous island where, in the 15th century, Louis XI built an eye-catching church beside a cliff.

RESTAURANT
Les Tonnelles
Béhuard
℘ 41.72.21.50
Rural restaurant on what is perhaps the most beautiful of the Loire islands. Affordable menus and wines mainly from Anjou.

Roche-aux-Moines.
Château d'Epiré (Epiré) This wine estate, which dates from 1640, has been in the hands of the same family since 1749. The Savennières produced here is set apart by an intense aroma, a firm structure and high quality. Sometimes a semi-dry is also made.

Clos de la Coulée Serrant
(Savennières) Organically worked, partially steep vineyard with old vines. The (expensive) wines require time and, after a while, acquire a marvellous aroma.
Domaine aux Moines (Savennières) Superb Roche-aux-Moines.

Saumur is dominated by its castle high on a hill.

HOTELS
Anne d'Anjou
32 Quai Mayaud
Saumur
✆ 41.67.30.30
Good hotel with 45
comfortable rooms
starting at FF 260. It is
situated on the quay,
below the castle. Pri-
vate car park. From the
rear of the hotel you can
walk through to the *Les
Ménestrels* restaurant
(41.67.71.10), which is
tastefully furnished.
Excellent cuisine (much
fish) and a wine list of
numerous regional
wines. Very good menu
at about FF 200.

SAUMUR

The silhouette of *Saumur*, 'the jewel of Anjou', is
dominated by an impressive castle built of white
tufa, which stands on a steep hill above the city.
The fortress was built about 1230, is flanked by
towers and has a medieval square form. At the
end of the 14th century Louis I of Anjou changed
it from a military bulwark into a lovely palace.
Other renovations would follow; for example,
King René embellished the interior in the 15th
century. The present building looks more sombre
than five or six centuries ago, but inside there is
much to be enjoyed because three museums have
been housed in the castle. The Musée d'Arts
Décoratifs exhibits French arts and crafts from

RECOMMENDED PRODUCERS
BRÉZÉ
Château de Brézé A range of quality,
with Saumur Brut, aromatic Saumur
Blanc, Saumur Rouge and semi-sweet
Coteaux de Saumur. Fantastic castle.
CHACÉ
Clos Rougeard Various sorts of Saumur-

Champigny, including the strong Le Bourg.
**Compagnie Française des Grands
Vins** Owned by Martini and producer of,
among others, the Saumur Brut Cadre
Noir.
Domaine des Galmoises Small estate,
high quality (as shown in the Saumur-
Champigny).

the whole country, including wall tapestries and porcelain. The Musée du Cheval is devoted to all possible aspects of equestrianism and the history of the local riding school is depicted. The Musée de la Figurine-Jouet is situated in a powder magazine and exhibits dolls and toys. Finally, the view across Saumur and the Loire valley will never be forgotten.

The oldest church in this city of around 35,000 inhabitants is the Notre-Dame-de-Nantilly, on the south side of the castle. The oldest section is 12th-century. Apart from other religious art treasures the gobelins (16th- and 17th-century) are worth looking at. Two other churches, both closer to the Loire, are Saint-Pierre (12th-century in origin, Baroque façade, wall tapestries) and the dome-shaped Notre-Dame-des-Ardilliers (17th-century, with a beautiful altar). In the centre of Saumur, which is partially car-free, you will find half-timbered houses (next to the church of Saint-Pierre) and fine buildings, such as the classically designed theatre and the 16th-century city hall which is partially built in the Gothic style and also fortified. The latter two buildings are

Auberge du Thouet
Chacé
☏ 41.52.97.02
Rural simplicity: 14 rooms starting at about FF 170. Regional menus start at less than FF 100.

Hôtel Le Bussy
Montsoreau
☏ 41.51.70.18
Only 15 rooms, but try to get one at the rear. Adequate comfort. Prices start at about FF 150. In the *Diane de Meridor* restaurant it is best to eat à la carte because the standard menu is somewhat ordinary.

Le Clos des Bénédictins
Saint-Hilaire-Saint-Florent
☏ 41.67.28.48

In Souzay-Champigny there is an ancient bell tower.

CHAINTRES
Château de Chaintres A 16th-century building where good white Saumur and Saumur-Champigny are made.
Domaine Filliatreau Large wine estate equipped with stainless steel fermentation tanks. Three sorts of Saumur-Champigny: Jeunes Vignes, Vieilles Vignes and Lena Filliatreau. Very reliable.

CHAMPIGNY
Clos des Cordeliers In the aromatic Saumur-Champigny you can taste small, red fruits.

DAMPIERRE-SUR-LOIRE
Yves et Gérard Drouineau Pleasing red

Good place to eat in Saumur.

Peacefully situated (along the D 751), on a hill (good view). The 24 rooms cost about FF 250 or more. It is also a restaurant. Swimming pool.
La Croix Blanche
Fontevraud-l'Abbaye
☎ 41.51.71.11
Nice hotel with two dozen rooms starting at about FF 200. Menus start at about FF 100.
Le Prieuré
Chênehutte-les-Tuffaux
☎ 41.67.90.14
Luxurious hotel, situated in a former priory. About 30 rooms starting at around FF 550. Excellent cuisine (menus start at about FF 250). Swimming pool, tennis court.

beside the Loire quay. The west side of Saumur is dominated by the Cadre Noir cavalry school, whose barracks are surrounded by large lawns. The city has devoted two museums to the military. The Musée de la Cavalerie displays the history of the French cavalry, and in the Musée des Blindés more than 700 tanks and associated equipment have been brought together.

From Saumur various excursions are possible. One could go in a northwesterly direction along the Loire. The first village is *Saint- Hilaire-Saint-Florent*. Gigantic quarries are found here, from which the stone was used for the construction of houses, churches and castles. Nowadays the caves are used for the storage of wine. It was a Belgian, Jean Ackerman (1788-1866), who was the first in Saumur to make a sparkling wine in the Champagne manner. This took place in 1811. No more than 40 years later others began to follow his example, which resulted in more and more caves at Saint-Hilaire-Saint-Florent being turned into wine cellars. In the rue Jean Ackerman you will find one wine-house after another, and most of them can be visited. On the square above the cellars of Bouvet-Ladubay there is the attractive little church of Saint-Hilaire-Saint-Florent (with heads above the portal), and also the Musée du Masque. This houses masks from the time of the Romans to present-day Hollywood. Near this

Saumurs and a Saumur Blanc of top quality.
Château de Hureau One of the best estates. Exemplary wines, white as well as red (Saumur-Champigny).
DISTRÉ
Domaine des Hautes Vignes The Fourrier family makes, among others, a

delicious Saumur Blanc, Crémant de Loire and red Cuvée du Fief aux Moines.
MONTREUIL-BELLAY
Château de la Durandière Modern equipment. Be sure to try the rosé.
Château de Montreuil-Bellay The castle owns a small vineyard, from which come a firmly structured red Saumur and

wine village the interesting Musée du Champignon can be visited, as well as the Ecole Nationale d'Equitation, France's national riding school. The stables of the Cadre Noir, with room for 1,200 horses, are situated there. The road along the Loire runs by way of *Chênehutte-les-Tuffeaux* and its high-class hotel to *Trèves*. Near the Romanesque church there is a 'donjon' (keep) from the 15th century. In *Gennes*, at the end of this journey, it is possible to visit a Gallic-Roman amphitheatre, as well as an archaeological exhibition (Château la Roche). Four dolmens can be seen around this village.

The excursion in a southerly and easterly direction takes longer. In *Bagneux*, a suburb of Saumur, the Musée du Moteur has been housed in the technical lyceum. In the same municipality and in strong contrast to the museum, is a 5,000-year-old dolmen 23 metres high, which makes it the largest in France. In *Distré* (further south, along the N 147) is a partially Romanesque church where, in 1668, a priest is said to have shown Jesus to his congregation in visible, human form, in a sacrificial bread. Furthermore, there are the remains of ramparts, the fountain of Saint-Martin, windmills and a dolmen (south side). By making a small detour via *Courchamps*, an elongated, old village on the crest of a hill, you can drive to *Montreuil-Bellay*. The castle there is

Hôtellerie Prieuré Saint-Lazare
Fontevraud-l'Abbaye
☎ 41.51.73.16
Reached by way of an automatic gate and situated in the former priory of the abbey. Comfortable rooms (50) at prices starting at about FF 350. It is also a restaurant.

Saint-Pierre
Saumur
☎ 41.50.33.00
Rather new hotel that is situated on a corner of the road to the castle, not far from the city

Château de Villeneuve in Souzay-Champigny.

centre, although it is still rather peaceful. 14 pleasant rooms offering more than adequate comfort. Prices start at about FF 300. No restaurant.

also a small amount of white.
Lycée Agricole From its own land this educational institution makes an attractive, white Saumur, a supple red and a Crémant de Loire.

PARNAY
Domaine du Val Brun Striking Crémant de Loire (with chardonnay, five years old),

tasty Saumur-Champigny Vieilles Vignes and Coteaux de Saumur.
Château de Targé Aromatic Saumur-Champigny (which can age). The cellars are modern. For 300 years the castle has been owned by the same family. Romanesque clock tower near the small graveyard.

RESTAURANTS

Auberge de l'Abbaye
Fontevraud-l'Abbaye
℃ 41.51.71.04
Cosy village inn where you can enjoy a tasty menu for less than FF 100. Traditional cuisine: much fish with *beurre blanc*

Les Chandelles
Saumur
℃ 41.67.20.40
Rather inventive cuisine

partially 11th-century but later, elegant sections were added, including a church with a 15th-century oratory and frescos from the same period. The collection of furniture is 17th- and 18th-century. The city centre, which is for a large part surrounded by ramparts, has many beautiful buildings. In the Grange à Dimes there is a Musée des Arts et Traditions and in the rue Dovalle the birthplace of the poet Charles Dovalle (1807-29). Near the Porte Saint-Jean, just outside the ramparts, hundreds of fish swim in

The castle of Montreuil-Bellay.

an aquarium, including many freshwater fish from the Loire area. Part of the aquarium is the Musée Paysan, which displays the rural life of the past. To the west of Montreuil-Bellay is the pilgrimage resort *Le Puy-Notre-Dame*. In the church, with its striking spire, a relic, brought back from the first crusade, has been on view for hundreds of years. It is a fragment of the silk sash worn by the Virgin Mary. This valuable item is said to aid the fertility of women. The village is France's largest producer of cultivated (cave) mushrooms. Now drive in a northeasterly direction to *Brézé*, where

based on market-fresh ingredients with, as a result, frequently changing menus (starting at about FF 165). Romantic interior.

LE PUY-NOTRE-DAME
Château de Beauregard Red and white Saumur, both have charm.
Clos de l'Abbaye Good Coteaux de Saumur and a red Cuvée des Chanoines which profits from ripening in the bottle.
Domaine de la Renière Wood-lagered Saumur Rouge and a nice Blanc.

SAINT-CYR-EN-BOURG
Co-operative A large producer with high standards. Many different wines, including various sorts of Crémant de Loire, Saumur Blanc, Saumur Rouge and Saumur-Champigny.
Domaine de Nerleux Extensive wine estate with a pure, floral Saumur Blanc, a

the Château de Brézé is situated. This has the deepest moat in all France. The stained-glass windows of the church take wine as their theme. The co-operative of *Saint-Cyr-en-Bourg* has wine cellars about 13 kilometres long. They can be visited by car. *Chacé* harbours the Musée du Champigny, where all stages of viniculture are brought to life. Apart from ordinary red Saumur, there is also Saumur-Champigny, which can only be made in seven municipalities (including Saumur itself). For the most part the vineyards are situated on a calcareous plateau to the east of Saumur. In general Saumur-Champigny has somewhat more depth, flesh and fruit than Saumur Rouge. The most important grape for both of them is cabernet franc, with or without the addition of cabernet sauvignon. The chenin blanc is used for the often very dry Saumur Blanc as well as for the rather rare, semi-sweet Saumur Coteaux de la Loire. For dry wines a small portion of chardonnay and/or sauvignon is also permitted. There is also a rosé; it is called Cabernet de Saumur. France's most often produced sparkling wine, after Champagne, is Saumur Brut. This can use ten different grapes as a base, white as well as red. Another effervescent wine is Crémant de Loire, for which stricter norms hold, with, as a result, a somewhat higher price, a much lower production and a much more limited reputation. The quality, though, can surpass that of Saumur Brut.

From *Chacé* it is not far to the wine village of *Varrains* (fine houses and a windmill where oak

La Croquière
Saumur
℃ 41.51.31.35
Affordable meals (the most expensive menu costs about FF 150) of a high quality. Regional and more modern dishes; nice wine list.

Les Délices du Château
Saumur
℃ 41.67.65.60
Impressive, stylishly furnished dining room in an annexe of the castle. The cuisine is perhaps even better here than in *Les Ménestrels* (of the *Anne d'Anjou* hotel). Fish prepared with Saumur-Champigny is often on the menu. Menus start at FF 170. A less expensive lunch menu during the week.

Le Gambetta
Saumur
℃ 41.67.66.66
Locally very respected place for lunch. Classic interior and cuisine. There is a menu from around FF 100 which, as desired, can consist of three or four courses (FF 20 difference). What's more, there is also a quick lunch menu for about FF 80. Interesting wine list. Terrace and garden.

Crémant which contains 30% chardonnay and a superior Saumur-Champigny Vieilles Vignes.

SAINT-HILAIRE-SAINT-FLORENT
Ackerman-Laurence Probably the largest producer of Saumur Brut. Property of Rémy-Pannier. Widely differing wines (also Crémants), with Cuvée Privée and Cuvée Jean-Baptiste as two of the best.

Bouvet-Ladubay Excellent Saumur Bruts, such as the Saphir, Cuvée Mlle Ladubay and Trésor. An Ecole de Dégustation is run here. Property of Taittinger.

Langlois-Chateau Subsidiary of the small Bollinger Champagne firm. Very

La Licorne
Fontevraud-l'Abbaye
℡ 41.51.72.49
Refined cuisine with much inventiveness, while the wine list is also worth a detour. Menus start at about FF 200.

Hostellerie Saint-Jean
Montreuil-Bellay
℡ 41.52.30.41
Pleasant place for lunch where the owner himself cooks. The dishes are rather classic but with a modern touch. The least expensive menu costs around FF 100. Good Saumurs in the cellar.

TOURIST TIPS
- In the village of Le Coudray-Macouard, between Saumur and Montreuil-Bellay, there is a castle with 12th-century cellars that can be visited.
- Around 1530 the composer Clément Janequin was named pastor of Brossay (between Doué-la-Fontaine and Montreuil-Bellay), but it is uncertain whether he accepted the post.

bark is tanned), from where a narrow road runs to the hamlet of *Chaintré* (houses from the 17th and 18th centuries) and then to *Dampierre-sur-Loire* (14th-century church). You will remain on the wine plateau by turning right before the village, in the direction of *Souzay-Champigny*. The little church here has a clock tower believed to be from the 11th century. Next to it is the entrance to the wine estate of Château de Villeneuve. In *Parnay* the church has Romanesque, Gothic and Renaissance elements. The Château de Targé wine estate deserves a visit for its architecture as well as for its wine. Across from the village there is an island in the Loire, which serves as a bird sanctuary for gulls and other birds. *Turquant* has an exhibition about cave dwelling. The Troglo'Tap in *Le Val Hulin* (just to the west) shows how, before the First World War, apples and other fruits were dried for use by sailors. Back on the

In Saint-Hilaire-Saint-Florent.

plateau there is the lonely, 15th-century *Moulin de la Herpinière*, on top of a cave with a small museum. Now go down to *Montsoreau*. The Caveau de la Motte contains a wine museum; there is also a mushroom museum and the

successful Crémants and a series of still wines from its own estate.
Veuve Amiot Correct Saumur Brut.
SAUMUR
Gratien & Meyer Very good sparkling wines, with the Cuvée Flamme (white and red) as the best. In Château Gratien, at the foot of the hill, is the International

School of Wine.
SOUZAY-CHAMPIGNY
Domaine de la Petite Chapelle Still Saumur, Crémant de Loire.
Château de Villeneuve Aromatic Saumur-Champigny, Saumur Blanc.
VARRAINS
Domaine des Roches Neuves

history of the Moroccan-French 'Gums' (soldiers) can be seen in the local castle (15th-century). The church of Saint-Pierre dates from the 13th century. *Candes-Saint-Martin*, in the extension of Montsoreau, is a

The abbey of Fontevraud.

beautiful river village. Walk up from the attractive church in order to enjoy the view across the Loire and the Vienne, which flow together here. The last stop is *Fontevraud-l'Abbaye*. This gigantic abbey was founded in 1099 and offered lodgings to monks as well as nuns. It was ruled by an abbess (often of royal blood). The sick, lepers and penitent, fallen women were welcomed, which is why the kitchen was set up to serve around 500 meals. In the cloister four tombstones of Plantagenet queens have survived; three were made from tufa, the fourth from wood. The abbey – which served as a prison for generations – is nowadays used for cultural events and exhibitions.

- It is thought that the cellars of Gratien & Meyer originated as quarries to produce the building stone for the Château de Saumur.
- In Turquant a miniature train, in which adults can also ride, runs in the season.
- The castle of Montsoreau, which once had a moat with water from the Loire, was immortalised in La Dame de Montsoreau, a novel by Alexandre Dumas.
- Wine information can be obtained in the Maison du Vin de Saumur (25, rue Beaurepaire in the centre of Saumur).

Distinctive, crowned Saumur-Champigny La Marginale.
Domaine des Varinelles A Crémant with a lot of chardonnay and a delicious Saumur-Champigny Vieilles Vignes.

RELATED TO WINE
- The first weekend in April: wine fair in Saumur.
- The first Sunday in August: wine exchange in Montsoreau.
- Second weekend in September: Fête du Saumur-Champigny in Varrains. The La Commanderie du Taste-Saumur wine fraternity also holds a celebration then.

TOURAINE

The former province of Touraine now comprises the department of
Indre-et-Loire with parts of Loir-et-Cher and Indre. The area stretches
from the point where the Vienne flows into the Loire, until near Blois,
dozens of kilometres to the east. The city of Tours forms the middle
point. Touraine is called 'the garden of France' because of its extensive
forests, green valleys, numerous orchards and fertile fields. It also has a
mild climate: the winters are seldom really hard, the summers almost
never really hot. It is no wonder that French monarchs and rich
aristocrats chose this area to build their castles, usually for themselves
but also frequently for their mistresses. The majority of the buildings
had no military function but served as pleasure mansions. Most of
them are well preserved, with the result that Touraine seems like a
gigantic open-air museum with the world's largest collection of castles.
Touraine has also produced famous figures, including the philosopher
Descartes (1596-1650) and the writers Rabelais (1494-1553), Ronsard
(1524-85) and Honoré de Balzac (1799-1850). The latter wrote: 'Shame
on him who does not admire my joyous, my beautiful, my brave
Touraine, with its seven valleys in which water and wine flow.' A few
of the most important valleys to which Balzac refers, are those of the
Cher, the Indre, the Loir, the Vienne and, indeed, the Loire itself.
Wine has been made along the banks since time immemorial. A
pioneer role in this was played by Martinus of Tours – later Saint
Martinus or Saint Martin. After France's first monastery was founded,
he was named archbishop of Tours in 371. He stimulated winegrowing
after his donkey broke some twigs from a grapevine. It seemed that the
remaining twigs bore much more fruit than previously – thus,
according to legend, the importance of pruning was discovered.
Nowadays Touraine makes a lavish amount of wines; the appellations
of the most interesting are mentioned in this guide.

HOTELS

Chéops
Chinon
℅ 47.98.46.46
Modern, comfortable
hotel with a pyramid-
shaped main building.
The 55, modernly
furnished rooms – more
than half of them with a
view of the castle –
start around FF 330. It is
also a restaurant. The
Chéops is situated on
the south bank of
Chinon.

Chris'Hôtel
Chinon
℅ 47.93.36.92
Pleasant rooms without
frills and often with
floral wallpaper. The
baths are sometimes
quite small. Friendly
service and a
newspaper arrives with
breakfast. No
restaurant. Parking in
front of the door, on the
place Jeanne d'Arc. The
40 rooms start at about
FF 250.

Château de Danzay
Beaumont-en-Véron
℅ 47.58.46.86
Luxurious establishment
on a peaceful wine
plateau. The castle is
15th-century and the
10 rooms (starting at
FF 600) are stylishly
furnished. It is also a

Chinon and its castle.

CHINON

The contrast could not be greater between
France's first atomic plant, built along the Loire,
and the still almost medieval Chinon, some 12
kilometres to the south along the Vienne. Within
15 minutes you drive at least 500 years back in
time. Chinon stands caught between a steeply
rising, elongated hill and the river bank. First the
Gauls and later the Romans built a fortification
on the hill. In the 10th century, a castle arose
here, built by Thibault the Deceiver, Duke of
Blois and Lord of Chinon. Halfway into the 12th
century the fortress became the property of
Henry Plantagenet, the future Henry II of
England. He choose Chinon as one of his most
important residences, rebuilt the castle and died
here in 1189. His son Richard Coeur-de-Lion,
who stayed here often, also ended his days here,
ten years later. In 1205, after a siege lasting a year,

RECOMMENDED PRODUCERS
BEAUMONT-EN-VÉRON
Domaine du Colombier Various red
Chinons, with Vieilles Vignes the best.
Château de Coulaine A 15th-century
location where a deep-coloured, very
fruity Chinon is made.
CHINON

Domaine de l'Abbaye Large wine
estate. You absolutely must taste the
Clos de la Collardière here.
Couly-Dutheil Wine firm and owner of a
few dozen hectares of vineyards. Each of
the Chinons is of exemplary quality, with
the Clos de l'Echo the highlight. The
cellars are three storeys high and have

the bulwark was stormed by the French, bringing an end to the reign of the Plantagenets in Touraine. Afterwards French kings would now and then reside here. One of them was Charles VII who was driven out of Paris in 1418. On 8 March 1429 he received a visit from the 17-year-old Joan of Arc, who asked him for troops with which to break the English siege of Orléans and convinced him to let himself be crowned in Reims. The grandeur that the castle knew under Charles VII, who held court there, has vanished, as have several buildings, because in the 17th century Cardinal Richelieu built a city named after himself – for which stones from Chinon's castle were used. All that remains of the once proud bulwark are ramparts, a few dwellings and various towers that stretch along a length of 400 metres. In the Tour de l'Horloge the Musée Jeanne d'Arc is housed, with, among other things, a

Château de la Grille, near Chinon.

In Cravant-les-Coteaux.

restaurant (dinner only). Menus start at about FF 270. Swimming pool.
Diderot
Chinon
☏ 47.93.18.87
Situated just outside the centre, on the east side. The 25 rooms are adequately furnished. Prices start at about FF 200. No restaurant.
La Giraudière
Beaumont-en-Véron
☏ 47.58.40.36
Peace is assured: this hotel, which is housed in a 17th-century mansion, is situated in the middle of a park rich in flowers. About 25 rooms with rural comfort, starting at about FF 200. Restaurant.

been carved out of the castle cliff.
Château de la Grille Situated along the road to Huismes and the property of the Gosset Champagne house. Modernly equipped cellar, storage area in a tufa stone quarry and very high quality. The castle is 15th- to 19th-century. Notice the hedges, which have been cut into curious shapes (e.g. an elephant). The wine bottles are an old-fashioned shape.
CRAVANT-LES-COTEAUX
Domaine Bernard Baudry Very reliable. There is a young wine, which can be drunk quickly, Vin de Pâques, and a wine to be put aside, Les Grézeaux.
Domaine des Falaises Well-structured,

Le Haut-Clos
La Roche-Clermault
✆ 47.95.94.50
Rather small hotel with
14 pleasant rooms, built
on a hill on the south
bank. You will recognise
it by a small tower. In
the restaurant the
specialities are fish and
grillades of meat.
Menus start at around
FF 100.

Château de Marçay
Marçay
✆ 47.93.03.47
Castle hotel with a wide
reputation; many
famous people have
stayed here. Wonderful
park, private vineyard,
tennis court, heated
swimming pool.
Fashionably decorated
rooms, 34 in number,
starting at about FF 500.
Excellent cuisine (menus
begin at around FF 250;
less-expensive lunch
menu through the week)
and a very large wine
list. When the weather
is good you can dine on
the terrace.

RESTAURANTS
Au Bon Accueil
Crouzilles
✆ 47.58.57.92
Rural inn, near the local
Romanesque church.
You can eat a filling,

Attractive street in Chinon.

reconstruction of her meeting with Charles VII.

Chinon ('petite ville, grand renom') has a centre that is full of mansions and other buildings from the 13th and up to and including the 16th centuries. Some were built in the half-timbered style. Most of them are situated in and around the rue Voltaire and the rue Haute-Saint-Maurice which is an extension of the former. Memories of Chinon of old and of inland shipping in the 19th century are brought together in the Musée du Vieux Chinon et de la Batellerie, while 14 mechanical dolls depict wine activities in the Musée animée du Vin et de la Tonnelerie. Visitors are also given wine to taste. The chapel of Sainte-Radegonde (6th, 11th, 12th, 13th centuries), which was partially carved from a cliff, houses the Musée des Arts et Traditions (arts and crafts) and has wall paintings that depict the Plantagenets. Chinon also has three old churches. The collegiate church of Sainte-Mexme is in part Carolingian and Romanesque, with 11th-century sculptures against the façade. In 1429 Joan of Arc prayed in the dome-shaped Saint-Maurice (12th-16th centuries), and the

tasty red wine.
Domaine de la Perrière The first wine estate to change over totally to stainless steel fermentation tanks (in 1974). Colourful, fruity Chinons. The Jeunes Vignes as well as the Vieilles Vignes deserve a recommendation.
Serge et Bruno Sourdais Of the various

sorts of red Chinon, the Les Clos and Les Cornuelles are two of the most attractive.
Gérard Spelty Red Clos de Neuilly.
CROUZILLES
Domaine Coton Frequently crowned wines, full of fruit.
LIGRÉ
Domaine Dozon Thanks to many old

15th-century Saint-Etienne not only has a flamboyant portal but also a marble statue of Joan of Arc. Another statue of this girl from Lorraine, this time in bronze, stands on the market square named after her on the east side of the village. Starting from Chinon, a pleasant half-day trip can be made. Take the D 21 in an easterly direction and, in the wine village of *Cravant-les-Coteaux*, turn left to the Vieux Bourg. It has a Carolingian church from the 9th, 10th and 11th centuries. A road surrounded by grapevines runs from Cravant to *Panzoult*. A little further on along the road you will see an

Château de Danzay is a hotel.

enormous dovecot from the 17th century. Now drive past l'Ile-Bouchard to *Crouzilles*, in order to take a peek at the compact, Romanesque church from 1045 and the statues on its walls. Go back to *l'Ile-Bouchard* and cross the Vienne to the village centre. Here stands the church of Saint-Gilles

tasty meal for FF 100 or less (leg of lamb, boar, etc.). It is also a bar and hotel.

Auberge Cravantaise
Cravant-les-Coteaux
✆ 47.98.40.82
Suitable for a simple, affordable midday meal (under FF 100). There are also 10 simple hotel rooms. Situated directly on the road.

Hostellerie Gargantua
Chinon
✆ 47.93.04.17
The cuisine and ambiance here are traditional and solid (*coq au vin de Chinon*). The staff sometimes walk around in medieval costume. At least 10 good hotel rooms, starting at about FF 250.

l'Océanic
Chinon
✆ 47.93.44.55
In the heart of Chinon, this is a good place for fish lovers. Oysters are often on the menus, which start at about FF 100. Flowery table linen.

Au Plaisir Gourmand
Chinon
✆ 47.93.20.48
Small business with a chic, but not really cosy, interior and indirect

vines in the vineyard the Clos du Saint-au-Loup has a taste with depth.
Château de Ligré A 19th-century castle where white, rosé and red Chinon is produced. The red Roches-Saint-Paul is often exquisite.
Domaine de la Noblaie A red quite rich in tannin and a charming white Chinon.

PANZOULT
Domaine de Beauséjour A vineyard comprising one plot, giving a pleasing Chinon which, as is shown by the older vintages that are available, can also ripen well.
Domaine du Roncée Various sorts of red Chinon, including the expressive Clos

neon lighting. You get the urge to whisper. The cuisine, however, is excellent and refined, with a classic undertone (*mousseline de brochet au coulis de homard*). The seasonal menus start at around FF 180. On the wine list there are numerous red Chinons and other wines from the Loire area.

TOURIST TIPS

- In the tourist season, a steam locomotive with old carriages runs to Richelieu.
- Richelieu really deserves a visit because it is a 17th-century masterpiece of urban architecture. La Fontaine called it 'the most beautiful village in the universe'.
- Apart from its 15th-century castle hotel, Marçay also has a Romanesque church, while the village itself is also beautiful.
- From Easter until into September it is possible to make a round trip through Chinon on a small train. The journey lasts about 30 minutes.

(partially 12th-century) and that of Saint-Maurice (15th-century clock tower and, inside, beautiful wood carving). The village also has the ruins of the 11th-century priory of Saint-Léonard and a handicraft museum, the Musée du Bouchardais. In *Tavant*, just to the west, the Romanesque church of Saint-Nicolas has fantastic frescos from the 10th and 12th centuries (in the crypt and above the altar). After *Sazilly*, where there is a church from the 12th century, you pass the castle of Bretignolles which is surrounded by a wall and, unfortunately, cannot be visited. *Ligré* (exit D 26) has a large dolmen and the church here is partially 12th-century. Back on the D 749, take the road to *La Divinière*, where, around 1490, Rabelais was born. His modest house is now a museum. In nearby *Seuilly*, the imposing Château de Coudray-Montpensier can only be viewed from outside. In

Wine plateau near Beaumont-en-Véron.

des Maronniers.

SAVIGNY-EN-VÉRON

Jean-Maurice Raffault Very old family estate with land in seven municipalities. The red Chinons have a long life, in particular the Les Galluches.

Domaine Olga Raffault Rather supple, fruity red Chinons and a good-natured

white.

Domaine du Raffault Aromatic, firm red Chinon with fruit, flowers and wood. It is also the property of a Raffault, Raymond.

SAZILLY

Charles Joquet In a progressive and well-organised manner, a painter makes a number of red Chinons here, which are

Dovecote near Panzoult.

this village you will also find an old abbey (founded in 1100, rebuilt in the 15th century). The villages north of Chinon are mainly worth a visit because of the wine estates. It is particularly pleasant to tour around *Beaumont-en-Véron*, where a jumble of vineyards flourish. Using the cabernet franc as a base, mainly red wines are made in Chinon. The best have an elegant firmness, the fruitiness of small, red fruits and berries, plus sufficient tannin to ripen for years. In quality they belong among the best red wines of the entire Loire valley. A certain amount of rosé and a little white Chinon are also made.

- On the quay at Chinon, close to the place Général de Gaulle, there stands a statue of Rabelais.
- Chinon holds a very popular medieval market on the first weekend in August.
- On the third Saturday in August the 19th century comes to life by means of the Marché à l'Ancienne.
- A few times every year Chinon organises a concours hippique (often on or around 15 August).
- The name Saint-Maurice (after whom churches were named in Chinon and l'Ile-Bouchard) refers to a hermit of the 5th century who resolved a desperate shortage of water by praying for a rainstorm – which came.

vinified by the field and can often ripen in the bottle for at least a decade. Two of the finest wines are the Cuvée des Varennes du Grand Clos and Clos de la Dioterie.

RELATED TO WINE

- In the first or second weekend of March there is a wine fair in Chinon.
- 1 May: wine fair in Panzoult.
- Easter Sunday: fair of the left-bank wines in Sazilly.
- Ascension Day: wine fair in Cravant-les-Coteaux.
- Second weekend in August: open cellars in Panzoult during a wine fair.

HOTEL
Château de Rochecotte
Saint-Patrice
© 47.96.21.28
This charming castle, which once belonged to Talleyrand, is situated in Saint-Patrice, the eastern municipality of the Bourgueil area. In the 22 comfortable rooms, old and modern furniture is mixed.

BOURGUEIL

The village of Bourgueil acquired stature in 990, when an important Benedictine abbey was founded by Emma, the daughter of Thibault the Deceiver, Count of Blois. In this way Emma did penance for the revenge she had taken on the mistress of her husband. For centuries the abbey has served as a refuge for the local population in times of disaster. There is little left of the original building: first the English set it on fire and it was later partially destroyed during the French Revolution. Still, the total complex remains impressive. The cellars are 13th-century, as is the Porte de la Crosse. The cloister partially dates from 1472 but the majority

The abbey at Bourgueil.

of the buildings are 17th- and 18th-century. Among other things, visitors can see a diorama about the daily life of the monks. It is possible that it was near this abbey that the cabernet franc was planted for the first time, probably by Abbot Baudry, around 1100. Coming from the Bordeaux region and being delivered by way of the Breton port of Nantes, the grape received the

Prices start at about FF 550. Park, fine terrace and its own restaurant (menus start at about FF 200).

RESTAURANTS
l'Ecu de France
Bourgueil
© 47.97.70.18

RECOMMENDED PRODUCERS
BENAIS
Domaine de le Chanteleuserie
Delanou Frères
Pierre-Jacques Druet Top class.
Domaine Hubert
Paul Maître
Jacques Morin

Domaine Pierre Gauthier
BOURGUEIL
Clos de l'Abbaye/G.A.E.C. de la Dîme
Yannick Amirault
Audebert et Fils
Domaine de la Coudraye
Domaine des Galluches
Domaine des Geslets

Cafe in Saint-Nicolas-de-Bourgueil.

nickname 'breton'. In Chinon, however, it is claimed that the variety was first brought to the Loire area in 1631 by one of Cardinal Richelieu's stewards, an abbot named Breton.

Whatever the truth may be, the cabernet franc is still planted in abundance in and around Bourgueil. The locally made red (and rosé) wine must be made up of 90 per cent of it. The only other grape permitted is the cabernet sauvignon. The same conditions also hold for red (and rosé) Chinon but these wines are different in character. Bourgueil usually tastes somewhat sturdier and has, in addition to a raspberry-like fruit tone, quite a bit of tannin, which means that it generally needs about five years to develop. Chinon tends to be slightly more fine, with, apart from fruit, some hint of small flowers, such as violets. In both areas, however, there are wines that cannot, or can barely, be differentiated from each other even by professionals. Saint-Nicolas-de-Bourgueil is a small area that borders on the western part of Bourgueil. A Saint-Nicolas generally has less tannin than a characteristic Bourgueil but there are also Bourgueils which can be drunk relatively quickly, above all if they

In a street between the abbey and the church. Regional, traditional cuisine (leg of lamb, shoulder of lamb) and friendly prices (menus begin under FF 100). It is also a simple hotel.

Auberge de Touvois
Touvois
℗ 47.97.88.81
Situated well over 4 kilometres north of Bourgueil, along the D 749. Rustic interior. Regional dishes (such as *coq au vin de Bourgueil*). Menus start at around FF 100. Nice wine list.

In Bourgueil.

TOURIST TIPS
• Saint-Nicolas-de-Bourgueil celebrates its village festival on the second Sunday after Easter.

Domaine de la Lande
INGRANDES-DE-TOURAINE
Domaine des Chesnaies/G.A.E.C.
Lamé-Delille-Boucard
Domaine de la Gaucherie/Domaine Régis Mureau
Nau Frères
Domaine des Ouches

SAINT-NICOLAS-DE-BOURGUEIL
Domaine du Bourg
Alain Caslot
Domaine de la Chevrette
Domaine de l'Epaisse
Vignoble de la Jarnoterie
Jacques Mabilau
G.A.E.C. Clos des Quarterons

The church in Restigné.

• At the end of October a chestnut market is held in Bourgueil.
• In some places in the Bourgueil area chambres d'hôte are available. Ask for information at the city hall in Bourgueil.

are made from the grapes grown on the same type of gravelly soil as in Saint-Nicolas-de-Bourgueil. Aside from its abbey, the village of Bourgueil has the church of Saint-Germain (12th-century, restored in the 19th) which has a marvellous choir. The market hall (market on Tuesdays) is situated near the building. Two kilometres north of Bourgueil is the Le Moulin Bleu, where tannic acid was formerly extracted from chestnut rind. Also on the northern side (follow the signs) is the Cave Touristique, a gigantic cave cellar. You can taste wine here and there is a collection of old wine objects.

A few other villages belong to the appellation of Bourgueil. *Restigné* has the beautiful, small church of Saint-Martin, with an 11th-century nave, primitive Romanesque sculpture in the portal and a 13th-century choir. In the village there are various fine buildings, including Château de Louy (16th/17th-century, with a beautiful inner courtyard), the Manoir du Brûlon (15th-century, multi-angular stair tower, wall paintings) and the Manoir de la Platerie (17th/18th-century, with an orangery). The former Santi Nicolai, nowadays called *Saint-Nicolas-de-Bourgueil*, is dominated by its 19th-century church but, visually, hasn't much else to offer.

Domaine des Valettes
Clos du Vigneau

RELATED TO WINE
• On the first Sunday in February there is a wine fair in Bourgueil.
• At Easter a wine and livestock market takes place in Bourgueil, followed by

the annual village festival on Tuesday.
• On the Sunday after 14 July Saint-Nicolas celebrates its Fête des Vignerons.
• The middle of August: wine festival in Bourgueil.

TOURAINE AZAY-LE-RIDEAU

One of the most visited villages in Touraine is Azay-le-Rideau. This is not so much because of the place itself, although at the side of the rectangular village square there is a charming, winding, little street with a church from the 11th/13th century that has a Carolingian sculpture on the right façade. The most important tourist attraction, in fact, is the castle, which is a sublime example of Renaissance architecture. It was finished in 1529, over the remains of a fort which, together with the village itself, had gone up in flames about a century previously. This was an act of vengeance by the dauphin, who later became Charles VII, because, as he was passing through Azay in 1418, on his way from Chinon to Tours, he had been attacked by the garrison of Burgundians who were stationed there (and who had chosen the side of the English during the Hundred Years War). Charles had the whole garrison killed and burned the fort and the village, which led

Little street near the castle.

to the village being called Azay-le-Brulé for over a century. The new castle was built by Gilles Berthelot, the treasurer of Francis I. Two years before the mansion was completed, he and his wife fled to the north of France following a fraud scandal. Since 1905, the castle of Azay-le-Rideau (which was still being worked on in the 19th

RECOMMENDED PRODUCERS
AZAY-LE-RIDEAU
Château de l'Aulée This is the largest wine estate of the area and the property of the Deutz Champagne house. One of the wines produced here is a pure, white Touraine Azay-le-Rideau.
Robert Denis Small winegrower who makes excellent, distinctive wines, rosé as well as white (dry and semi-sweet). The semi-sweet version needs ageing. Or, as Denis himself said: 'Not until after 20 years do you see the sun in the glass.'
René Menard Miniscule production of white Azay-le-Rideau.
Pibaleau Père & Fils Dry rosé and

RESTAURANTS
l'Aigle d'Or
Azay-le-Rideau
℃ 47.45.24.58
The cuisine here is talented and creative, maintaining traditional values. Menus start at FF 150 and there is a less expensive lunch menu during the week. Young rabbit (*lapereau*) is often on the menu, as is fresh fish. Many regional wines. Two dining rooms and a garden.

L'Automate Gourmand
La Chapelle-St. Blaise
℃ 47.45.39.07
Small business built against a tufa cliff in a village straight across from Azay-le-Rideau, on the other bank of the Indre. Very carefully prepared cuisine. Excellent wine selection. There are lunch menus on weekdays for less than FF 100, starting at about FF 140 for an ordinary menu.

Les Grottes
Azay-le-Rideau
℃ 47.45.21.04
Situated on a street corner past the castle entrance and housed in a cave cellar where wine was formerly

century) has been the property of the French state. It is situated on an island in the Indre. Seen from certain corners of the surrounding park, it seems to float on the water like a large, fairy-tale yacht. The roof and spires of the four round towers are blue, while the building itself was constructed from white stone. Inside there is a

The castle stands on an island.

museum devoted to Renaissance art (furniture, Flemish wall tapestries). You will also find a kitchen with an enormous fireplace, and paintings, including a fascinating portrait of the half-dressed Gabrielle d'Estrées ('La Belle Gabrielle'), the favourite mistress of Henry IV. Together with seven other municipalities Azay-le-Rideau forms the appellation of Touraine Azay-le-Rideau. Its vineyards extend for only a few dozen hectares and only produce dry rosé and white wine. The latter can vary in taste from very dry to semi-sweet. The white Azay-le-

white Azay-le-Rideau, plus a few types of Touraine.

CHEILLÉE
La Cave des Vallées Stands out because of its refreshing, aromatic rosé.

VALLERES
Frédéric Hardy In this village between Azay and Villandry you will find a large range of wines produced by Hardy, including a dry, energetic rosé from Azay.

The entrance on the castle.

Rideau can often be kept in the bottle without problems for two to three decades. The most interesting wine village, to the west of Azay, is *Cheillé*. The remains of a Gallic-Roman wine press have been found there. The Château de l'Isolette, situated nearby, is 16th-century; to a certain extent the architect was inspired by the castle of Azay-le-Rideau. East of Azay, *Saché* deserves a visit. The village itself is picturesque; in front of the Romanesque church is a striking and controversial construction by the 20th-century American artist Alexander Calder. Honoré de Balzac often stayed in the Château de Saché. This hard-working and productive author (1799-1850) wrote at least four of his works here, including the famous 'Les Lys dans la Vallée', which takes place in the Indre valley. The 16th-century castle serves nowadays as the Musée Balzac. You can visit the room where he worked, see portraits, writing materials, manuscripts and proofs, sometimes with hand-written corrections, as well as the printed texts.

stored. In the two charming rooms you eat by candlelight. Small menu for less than FF 100 (e.g. half a hare with pine nuts) but the menu starting at FF 130 offers tasty food that is great value for money (mousseline of pike, crayfish tails, etc.).

TOURIST TIPS
- From March to October: son et lumière near the castle of Azay-le-Rideau.
- Likewise in Saché, where, at the castle, a sound and light spectacle about Balzac and 'la vallée du lys' is presented (middle of July until the beginning of August).
- At the beginning of July there is an evening market in Azay, usually on the first Friday.
- At the end of October Azay holds an apple exchange.
- Azay-le-Rideau has a mini-golf course.
- 6 kilometres south of Azay is Villaines-les-Rochers, where many basketmakers are still active.

RELATED TO WINE
- On the square behind the village square of Azay-le-Rideau there is a small, modern tasting room belonging to the collective producers.
- Azay-le-Rideau has a wine fair during the last weekend in February.

TOURS

The heart of Tours, the capital of Indre-et-Loire, is situated between the Loire and the Cher, which flow together some 20 kilometres to the west. The place takes its name from the Gallic tribe of the Turones. During the Roman occupation an important encampment was founded here, which was called the Caesarodunum, the hill of the Caesar. After the Romans left, Tours gradually grew into a prosperous trading city – although it had its ups and downs because fighting often took place here. The last time this happened, Tours suffered major damage due to bombs during the Second World War. Fortunately, the old centre, Vieux Tours, was carefully rebuilt and restored. The town suburbs stretch out along the north bank of the Loire and the south bank of the Cher but for a tourist they are of no interest. Only the abbey of Marmoutier, on the northern bank of the Loire (between Tours and Rochecorbon, just past the viaduct of the *autoroute*), is worth a visit. It was founded around 375 by the archbishop of Tours, Martinus. The abbey was the most powerful in all France. Nowadays only a fraction of the former buildings remains. Parts of the monastic cells were carved from tufa stone, as were the graves.

After the death and canonisation of Martinus, Tours became a place of pilgrimage, which stimulated the growth of the city. The basilica named after Saint Martin, which, in the 5th century, was the first in the world, was rebuilt and enlarged in the 12th and 13th centuries. Only two towers and the tomb of the saint still remain from the original building. The white basilica stands in Vieux Tours, the old city area, west of the centre (between the extension of Pont Wilson and Pont Napoléon). You will find many half-timbered houses there, some of which have stepped gables. Place Plumereau, where cafe terraces are surrounded by narrow, half-timbered houses, is a charming square between the basilica and the Loire quay. In the same neighbourhood you will find the Musée du Gemmail (rue du Mûrier). Colourful mosaics and a special sort of glass are exhibited here. The rue du Commerce runs in an easterly direction by way of place Saint-Pierre. The Hôtel Gouïn, which has a marvellous 16th-century façade and houses a museum with artefacts that date back to the Gallic-Roman period, is here. Beside the museum is an excellent restaurant, La Rôtisserie Tourangelle, and next to this is a baker who sells delicious sandwiches. It is now only a few dozen metres to the rue Nationale, which cuts through the city from the Pont Wilson. Close to the junction with the rue du Commerce stands the abbey of Saint-Julien, built from grey stone, with a 13th-century monastery church (and behind it a rather large car park). In what was formerly the monastery garden, but is now a courtyard, a 16th-century, covered winepress can be seen. That it stands here is no coincidence because in the cellars of the abbey you will find the Musée des Vins de Touraine. It was opened in 1975 and contains a rich collection of wine articles. The Comité Interprofessionnel des Vins de Touarien, which supplies information about the regional wines, is situated next to it. In another monastery building, which is reached by means of a small bridge between shops on the rue Nationale, is the Musée du Compagnonnage. It is devoted to old crafts and their guilds, such as tanners and stone masons. On the other side of the rue Nationale the rue Commerce changes into the rue Colbert. By following this to the end you will come to the cathedral of Saint-Gatien. It was worked on

A timber-framed building in the centre.

for about 300 years from the 13th century, which explains the presence of various architectural styles. However, the Gothic façade gives a marvellously harmonious impression. Inside, among other things, the rose windows are a visual delight. The archipiscopal palace, next to the cathedral, houses the Musée des Beaux-Arts. This collection comprises numerous paintings dating from the Middle Ages to the 20th century, plus sculptures, ceramics and furniture. The giant cedar in the inner courtyard is almost two centuries old. By walking from the museum in the direction of the Loire, you soon arrive at the Palais Royal. This fortress, which has been repeatedly rebuilt, once offered lodging to Charles VII and his son Louis XI. The present occupants are 60 waxworks, which illustrate important moments from the history of Touraine. The museum is called Historial de Touraine. It deserves a visit if only to see the costumes.

HOTELS

HOTELS
Château d'Artigny
Montbazon
✆ 47.26.24.24
Regal accommodation
situated high on a
wooded hill. Tennis
courts, heated
swimming pool. About
50 rooms and suites, of
the highest standards,
starting at around FF
500. The restaurant is

Château de Chenonceau.

likewise of excellent
quality. Striking wine
collection. Menus start
at around FF 280
(inexpensive lunch menu
during the week).
**Domaine de
Beauvois**
Luynes
✆ 47.55.50.11
This is surrounded by a
wooded estate of 140
hectares with a round
tower in the middle.
About 40 superior,

THE WINE AREA OF TOURAINE

Wines with the appellation Touraine are
produced from a very extensive area (which looks
rather like a sloppy ink stain on the map) with
Tours as the middle point and the valleys of the
Cher, Indre, Loire and Vienne radiating out.
Pleasant, fruity red wines are made here, mainly
from gamay and cabernet franc, while the type of
the aforementioned varieties called Tradition is
usually mixed with cot (or
malbec). White wines mainly
come from the sauvignon (often
very aromatic, fresh and juicy) or
from the chenin blanc (or pineau
de la Loire), giving a softer,
sometimes even mild, taste.
There are also effervescent and
sparkling Touraines. The region
enjoys a growing reputation for
its wines but its castles are still
much more famous and it also contains many
other places of interest. The two routes that will
be described run past the most beautiful places
and the most important wine villages. The longer
route begins in *Chenonceaux*, where stands one of
France's most popular monuments, the Château
de Chenonceau; every year it attracts almost a
million visitors. It was completed in 1521. Later in
the same century it was extended by a two-storey
wing over the Cher. When Henry II ascended the
throne in 1547, he gave the castle to his mistress
Diane de Poitiers who was his elder by 20 years.

RECOMMENDED PRODUCERS
ANGÉ-SUR-CHER
Domaine de la Garenne Good Touraine
Sauvignon. The village is situated just
west of Pouillé.
CHENONCEAUX
Château de Chenonceau Exemplary
wines from their own castle vineyard.

Cheerful, sparkling, aromatic white (also
semi-dry), fresh rosé, fruity red. The best
red undergoes cask ripening. It has,
deservedly, won many awards.
Domaine des Acacias Quite a large
wine estate, where the fleshy Gamay
Prestige is mainly worth discovering.
MAREUIL-SUR-CHER

She had a marvellous ornamental garden laid out. After the death of Henry II in 1559, his wife, Catherine de Médicis, took her revenge and forced Diane to leave. In the castle

The castle in Selles-sur-Cher.

there are many marvellous rooms to be seen, while, in an annexe, a wax museum has been housed, which depicts four centuries of the castle's history. In the village of Chenonceaux is the partially 12th-century church of Saint-Jean-Baptiste. Its fonts were gifts from Catherine de Médicis. In *Chissay-en-Touraine*, upstream along the Cher, is the Fraise d'Or distillery. *Saint-Georges-sur-Cher*, on the other bank, has a Romanesque church with a gobelin inside it. *Montrichard* is dominated by the remains of a powerful keep. This offers a delightful view and houses a small museum of folkloristic and archaeological objects. Archaeological finds are also exhibited in the Château de Pont-Cher. There are quite a few 15th- and 16th-century houses in Montrichard and, on the Cher quay, the cave cellars of two wine merchants can be visited. In the church of Sainte-Croix (Romanesque portal) Louis XII married Joan of France in 1476, whom he would later repudiate

comfortable rooms. Prices start at about FF 500. Excellent restaurant, fantastic wine list. Menus start at around FF 180. Swimming pool, tennis court.

Le Bellevue
Montrichard
✆ 54.32.06.17
30 well-furnished rooms on the Cher (and a second, somewhat simpler hotel in the neighbourhood for boarders). Prices start at about FF 230. In the restaurant regional wines are served with regional dishes, such as *coq au vin de Touraine.*

Hôtel du Bon Laboureur et du Château
Chenonceaux
✆ 47.23.90.02

Domaine de la Renaudie A large range of wines, generally of high quality, such as Touraine Sauvignon, Touraine rosé and the red Touraine Tradition (from cabernet, cot, gamay).

G.A.E.C. du Clos Roche Blanche Attractive red wines, including a firm Tradition.

MONTHOU-SUR-BIEVRE
G.A.E.C. Louet-Arcourt On the way to Château du Gué-Péan you will get to know, among others, a successful Touraine Sauvignon, as well as rosé, red and sparkling wines from the same area.

MONTRICHARD
Paul Buisse The cave cellar of Caves de

Very reliable and comfortable establishment that has been run for generations by the same family.

The basilica and castle of Saint-Aignan.

Some of the 40 rooms are situated in an annexe. Prices start at about FF 300. Regionally oriented, reliable restaurant. When the weather is good, meals are served outside. Menus start at around FF 200. The castle is within walking distance.
Les Cèdres
Savonnières
© 47.53.37.58
Around 40 rooms in a beautiful building in the middle of a park. Prices start at about FF 290. Its restaurant is a famous

for Anne of Brittany. The church of Notre-Dame de Nanteuil, just ouside the village, is a place of pilgrimage; Louis XI had a chapel built in this 12th-, 13th- and 15th-century monument. About 12 kilometres south of Montrichard is *Montpoupon*. In the 15th-century castle a small hunting museum has been set up. Bourré, along the Cher, has a mushroom nursery in its caves; you can make a guided tour of one of them. On the west side of *Thésée*, the remains of a Gallic-Roman settlement from the 2nd century BC can be seen (with a *caveau* where, in the season, wine can be tasted). Finds from the excavation are exhibited in the town hall of this elongated wine village. From Thésée you could make a small trip to *Monthou-sur-Cher* (Romanesque church) and the Château du Gué-Péan which lies behind it. The château is marked by four low towers, one of which has a bell-shaped dome. The interior of this late-Renaissance building consists of salons with 17th- and 18th-century furniture and a library with autographed books. On the south bank of the Cher are the wine villages of *Pouillé* and *Mareuil-*

la Boule Blanche dates from 1878, but the firm itself was founded in 1905. It sells a series of high-quality wines from the Loire valley, including Cristal Buisse Touraine Sauvignon, red Touraine Cabernet, Chinon, Bourgueil and Saint-Nicolas-de-Bourgueil, as well as Vouvray Moelleux. It has its own land in Pouillé.

J.M. Monmousseau The neighbour of Buisse and also with large cave cellars. Specialises in good sparkling wines; one of the brands is Brut de Mosny. Aside from this, they sell still wines, such as Vouvray and Montlouis.
NOYERS-SUR-CHER
Domaine de Beauséjour Deserves a

The castle at Ussé.

sur-Cher (11th-century church). Further to the east, on the same bank, *Saint-Aignan* is the next stop. The 11th- and 12th-century basilica has colourful frescos in one of the chapels and in the Romanesque crypt. From the church a wide flight of stairs runs to the castle, which cannot be entered but may be viewed from its inner courtyard. It displays Renaissance and medieval elements and has an impressive staircase tower and an octagonal keep from the 19th century. The view is also worth seeing. Not far to the south of Saint-Aignan, white tigers, about 100 apes, approximately 300 species of birds (including endangered ones) and other animals have been brought together in the Zoo de Beauval. If you cross the Cher from Saint-Aignan, tourist information can be obtained at the Maison du Vin and the adjacent Maison du Tourisme. From Noyers-sur-Cher, a wine village with a 13th-century church, the D 675 runs in a northerly direction to *Contres,*

place among wine lovers, because the patron is also one. Much fish on the menus, which start at around FF 170. Swimming pool.

Le Clos du Cher
Noyers-sur-Cher
ℂ 54.75.00.03
Situated in a walled park near a roundabout. A dozen adequate rooms start at about FF 400. Opened in 1990. No restaurant.

Le Cheval Rouge
Villandry
ℂ 47.50.02.07
Country hotel with 20 pleasant rooms, close to the castle. Prices start at about FF 310. Ask for

An autumnal vineyard.

a room at the rear. The cuisine is rather traditional and prepared with care. Menus start at around FF 175. Good wine list.

recommendation for its white Touraine Sauvignon as well as for its red Touraine.
Domaine Lévêque
Domaine Michaud Touraine Sauvignon and a Touraine Cabernet well supplied with small red fruits.
OISLY
Confrérie des Vignerons de Oisly et

Thésée A firm that was founded in 1961 and is the property of a few dozen winegrowers. It is run energetically and is very quality-conscious. In the wide assortment there are brand-name wines as well as wines from individual estates. The average quality is high. A speciality is Touraine Sauvignon. Apart from the

Hôtel de France
Contres
© 54.79.50.14
Elongated building on a busy street. It has blue sun screens. The rooms have double glazing but on warm days you

where there are hotels. You could also turn off in Couddes to go to *Oisly*, one of the most important wine municipalities of the entire Touraine. It was in this region that the sauvignon grape was first planted. In the Domaine de la Presle, the Boucher family has set up a modest museum which contains old agricultural and winegrowing tools (rooms can also be rented here). This route could be concluded by driving by way of Pontlevoy to *Chaumont-sur-Loire*. On a hill above the village

Gallo-roman ruins in Thésée.

simply must take a room at the rear. Prices start at about FF 275. Rural dishes in the restaurant. Menus start at around FF 120.

Château de la Gondelaine
Contres
© 54.79.09.14
Fine establishment surrounded by a large park. Tennis court. About 20 rooms, starting at FF 400. Good restaurant where the cuisine is inventive.

and the nearby Loire stands the Château de Chaumont. It dates from the end of the 15th and beginning of the 16th centuries. With its sturdy round towers it looks very warlike, but the interior is Renaissance. Catherine de Médicis and her rival Diane de Poitiers both lived here at one time. Their rooms can be visited. The floors and wall tapestries of Chaumont command admiration, as do the 19th-century stables. There are numerous tree species in the park and an exhibition of garden design was held here in 1992.

A second, shorter route might begin in Tours but

normal Sauvignons, those of Domaine du Grand Cerf, Château Vallagon and Domaine de la Chatoire deserve attention. From the two latter properties there are also successful red wines, just like those from Domaine du Bouc. The red and white wines called Baronnie d'Aignan are made from three grape

varieties, while the red and white Cuvée C.M.S. have, respectively, pinot noir and chardonnay as their base. Finally, sparkling Crémant de Loire is also produced.

Domaine des Corillières The grandfather of owner Maurice Barbou was the first in Touraine to plant the

could also begin in Azay-le-Rideau, Chinon or Bourgueil. Take the D 7 from Tours to *Savonnières*. Near this village, which is Roman in origin (the name comes from *Saponaria*), there is a large complex of stalactite/stalagmite caves around an underground lake of over 2.5 kilometres in length. A Gallic-Roman cemetery has also been discovered here. In the caves there is a constant temperature of 14 degrees Celsius. Savonnières has a church dating from the 12th century and a presbytry from the 15th. Near the entrance to neighbouring *Villandry* stands the local castle. It was completed in 1536 and was the last of the large Renaissance castles to be built along the Loire. It was commissioned by Jean le Breton, minister of state under Francis I. The U-shaped castle has a fine inner courtyard and an interior that was restored in the 18th century and has, among other things, works by the Spanish masters. Still more impressive are the gardens, where a large variety of plants grow in the middle of geometrically laid-out paths and drives. The gardens are situated on four levels. On the highest level is a water garden, which feeds the moat as well as the fountain and irrigates all of the other gardens. The middle levels comprise

Asparagus is a regional speciality.

Menus start at FF 150.
Château du Gué-Péan
Monthou-sur-Cher
✆ 54.71.43.01
Here you lodge in a real monument (20 rooms) or in an annexe (11 rooms). Prices start at around FF 300 (twice as much as in the castle itself), including breakfast. It is situated in the middle of a 2,400-hectare forest. Menu, including wine, at around FF 230.

sauvignon. The white wines from the sauvignon are always a speciality of the estate but the other still wines also have their merits.
Domaine Octavie Winner of many medals, for, among other wines, the Touraine Sauvignon and red Touraine Tradition.

Domaine du Pré Baron One of Guy Mardon's best wines is Touraine Tradition.
Domaine de la Presle Not only a conscientious wine firm (red, white, rosé) but also houses a small agricultural and winegrowing museum, while rooms can also be rented.

Château de la Ménaudière
Montrichard
© 54.32.02.44
Stylish rooms, 25 in number, with modern comforts in a castle that is 15th-century in origin. Prices start at around FF 400. Tennis court. Park. Own restaurant. Menus start at around FF 260 (less expensive lunch during the week).

Moulin de la Reine
Thésée
© 54.71.41.56
Rather small hotel (15 rooms) but comfortable and with reasonable prices (starting at about FF 250). Simple, affordable restaurant,

Wine estate in Oisly.

Confrérie des Vignerons in Oisly.

flower and herb gardens, while the lowest level offers a bountiful harvest of flowers, vegetables and fruit, including orange pumpkins. On the southwest side of Villandry is the striking menhir of La Pierre aux Joucs; it stands at a height of almost 4 metres. It is about 20 kilometres along the Loire from Villandry to *Rigny-Ussé*. With its many towers and pointed roofs, Château d'Ussé looks like a fairy-tale castle. It is said to have inspired Charles Perrault to write *Sleeping Beauty*, in 1697. The largest part of this fortification dates from the 16th and 17th centuries, but a large number of its successive owners made changes. The halls, rooms and salons of the castle contain magnificent wall tapestries and marvellous furnishings. Dolls in historical costumes give the whole place an extra cachet. Sleeping Beauty has not been

POUILLÉ
Domaine de la Bergerie Delicious Cabernet.
Daniel Delaunay
Joël Delaunay Touraine Sauvignon, red Touraine Cuvée Prestige.
Jacky Marteau Enjoys an excellent reputation due to its Touraine Sauvignon

and Touraine Gamay.
Domaine de la Rochette
Domaine des Sablons Modernly equipped property which produces exquisite wines, such as Touraine Sauvignon, Touraine Gamay and Touraine Cabernet.
SAINT-GEORGES-SUR-CHER

forgotten either. Now drive back in the direction of Tours and turn off in Lignières-de-Touraine to *Langeais*, on the right bank of the Loire. You drive into the city by way of a beautiful suspension bridge. The local

Cave cellar in Montrichard.

castle has a sombre, medieval appearance, being partially 13th-century. Inside it is much less plain. You will find 13 rooms with furnishings from the 15th and 16th centuries, as well as a unique collection of wall tapestries from the same period. The oldest part of the castle is a keep built in 994. It is one of the first of its kind to have been built in stone; before this they had been built of wood. The rest of the castle dates from 1465: built by Louis XI who wished to have a fortress that would discourage the Bretons from going upriver. Ironically enough, Charles VIII, Louis's son, married the 15-year-old Anne of Brittany here in 1491 (in the room in which it took place the ceremony is now depicted using wax dolls). Across from the castle is a Renaissance house where Rabelais is said to have lodged. Langeais is known for its decorated and glazed earthenware. In the Musée des Outils et des Hommes, tools from the past have been

where local wines are served.

Domaine de la Tortinière
Montbazon
✆ 47.26.00.19
A small castle with about 20 charming, elegant rooms starting at about FF 450. Tennis court, swimming pool, large park. Refined cuisine. Menus start at around FF 270.

RESTAURANTS
La Botte d'Asperges
Contres
✆ 54.79.50.49
Rustic inn where regional asparagus is served when in season. Fish is also often served. Menus begin under FF 100. There are a few hotel rooms.

Jean-Claude Bougrier Wine firm offering a number of pleasant wines, including Touraine Sauvignon.
Domaine des Perrets About seven wines are successfully produced here (red, white – dry and semi-dry – plus rosé). Some are sold under the name of Domaine de la Billette, but have the same owner.
SAINT-ROMAIN-SUR-CHER
Jean-Claude Bodin Pleasing sparkling wine and a rather firm red Cabernet.
Maurice Cordier Reliable across the whole range.
Joël Louet
SOIGNS-EN-SOLOGNE

Hotel in Contres.

La Chancelière
Montbazon
☎ 47.26.00.67
Here you eat meals of
top quality amid a decor
that has many antiques.
In particular, delicious
dishes are made from
fish, crustaceans and
shellfish. Carefully
selected wine list.
Menus start at about
FF 300 (less-expensive
lunch menus during the
week). The antiques are
also for sale.

Hosten/Le Langeais
Langeais
☎ 47.96.70.63
Family business where
the cuisine is rather
classic. It is situated
near the castle. Meals
start at around FF 300. It
is also a small hotel.
Room prices start at
around FF 350.

Le Relais de Chasse
Saint-Aignan

collected. Along the road to
Saumur is the Musée du Cadillac,
entirely devoted to this American
make of car. It is now 5
kilometres, in an easterly
direction, to *Cinq-Mars-la-Pile*.
The last part of the name
commemorates a 30-metre-high
pillar dating from the Roman
period. It is thought to be a
memorial stone. Cinq-Mars is the name of the
castle (situated between the village and the
pillar). Of the castle two, round battle towers
from the 11th and 12th centuries still remain. You
can reach them by way of a bridge across the
castle moat. In the large hall of the eastern tower
there is an enormous fireplace. The castle – and
its destruction – are connected with the history
of Henri d'Effiat, Marquis of Cinq-Mars, who,
as a spy for Cardinal Richelieu, won the trust of
Louis XIII but afterwards betrayed Richelieu and,
as a result, ended his days on the scaffold. He was
22 years old. By following the Loire, *Luynes*
comes into
view after
about 10
kilometres.
This has a
completely
medieval-
looking
castle (15th-
century),

The castle of Chaumont.

Domaine de la Charmoise Not far from
the D 956, between Contres and
Chémery, an exemplary Sauvignon
Touraine and a few red and rosé Gamays
are produced on this estate. The quality is
excellent, even that of the Gamay
Primeur. The owner, Henri Marionnet, has
done much for the reputation of white and

red Touraine wines and is nowadays one
of the best known winegrowers in the
Loire valley.
THÉSÉE
Domaine du Haut Chesneau Touraine
Tradition.
Caves de la Ramée

Hotel restaurant in Langeais.

© 54.75.01.89
Not very memorable but the cuisine is tasty and at reasonable prices. The least-expensive menu costs about FF 100. Cosy interior.

Le Saint-Vincent
Oisly
© 54.79.50.04
Situated on a corner of the village square. Unpretentious interior but a surprisingly good cuisine and really good value for money. Menus begin under FF 100. Wild game when in season, likewise asparagus.

very massive, rectangular and flanked by round towers. Unfortunately, it cannot be visited. At least as impressive is the Gallic-Roman aqueduct on the northeast side of the village. It is constructed from stone pillars and a few arches are still intact.

In the middle of the westerly and easterly route through the wine area of Touraine, *Montbazon* is situated along the Indre. At the end of the 10th century a powerful, 30-metre-high keep was erected here. A statue of the Virgin Mary was placed high on the square construction, which has walls over 2 metres thick. Parts of the former fortress remain.

TOURIST TIPS
- Just to the southeast of Savonnières, near the hamlet of Miré, there is a golf course.
- In Savonnières, on the first weekend of August, a donkey weekend usually takes place.
- In the season a son et lumière show takes place near many of the castles.
- It is possible to make a balloon trip from Chenonceaux.

RELATED TO WINE
- In Tours-Fondettes, a suburb of Tours, a large, professional wine fair is held annually during the first half of February.
- At Easter there is a wine fair in Saint-Georges-sur-Cher.
- Thésée organises a wine fair on the first weekend in July.
- First Sunday in August: Fête du Sauvignon in Oisly.

♀ **HOTELS**
⌗ **Les Fontaines**
Rochecorbon
℡ 47.52.52.86
Charming hotel that is
run in a friendly manner.
Adequate comfort and,
when the weather is
nice, breakfast is served
on the terrace. Situated
in a walled park on the
Loire quay. No
restaurant. Prices start
at around FF 200.
**Domaine des Hautes-
Roches**
Rochecorbon
℡ 47.52.88.88
11 luxurious rooms, set
in a cliff wall and with a
view across the river.
Starting at around
FF 600. Excellent
restaurant where the
cuisine, in particular
fish, is refined. Menus
start at around FF 175.
**Château de
Jallanges**
Vernou-sur-Brenne
℡ 47.52.01.71
You lodge here in a
15th/17th-century
castle which stands
isolated on a plateau.
Six rooms starting at
around FF 650 (including
breakfast). In the
evening you can eat
with the owner and also
take a drive in a
carriage.

View of Vouvray from the Clos Baudoin.

VOUVRAY

In the past the wines of Vouvray enjoyed an
excellent reputation. In the 16th century,
Rabelais described them as made 'of taffeta' and
they were exported for hundreds of years.
Nowadays things are somewhat quieter around
Vouvray, because the reputation of the wine
declined in the course of this century, due to
inexpensive, average, semi-sweet wines without
much class
or
personality.
In the 1970s
and 1980s, a
number of
winegrowers
opted once
more for
quality, so

Château de Jallanges is also a hotel.

RECOMMENDED PRODUCERS
CHANÇAY
Domaine Vigneau-Chevreau A not-
too-dry Vouvray Sec and a beautiful
Moelleux.
NOIZAY
Alain Cruchet Taste the Moelleux.
Joël Cosme A complete range.

Jean Raimbault Successful Vouvray
Brut, while the Moelleux also tastes
delicious.
ROCHECORBON
Marc Brédif This firm is the property of
Patrick de Ladoucette (see Pouilly-Fumé).
Superior Pétillant and Brut.
Caves St. Roch Producer of the

Vouvray has again begun to acquire a name within and outside France. For Vouvray (always white) only one grape variety is permitted, the chenin blanc. It is mainly planted on calcareous plateaus of tufa. The number of types of wine made here from chenin is surprisingly large. Most producers make a Vouvray Sec (which can be very dry), a semi-dry and, in years with lots of sun, a Moelleux (sometimes from overripe grapes and luxuriantly sweet). There is also a sparkling Vouvray (made in the Champagne manner; often named Vouvray Brut) and Vouvray Pétillant. The latter type is even more difficult to make than Vouvray Brut and also requires a better base wine. The extra effort is well worthwhile, however, because a good Pétillant is a delight. Coming from Tours, by way of the northern bank of the Loire, *Rochecorbon* is the first wine village of the appellation Vouvray. It has had many names but, finally, the name of a knight called Corbon was chosen, who lived here around 1000. On a cliff above the village rises La Lanterne, a high, square tower from the 15th century. Beside this are the remains of a castle. The tower can be seen just before the turn-off to the village centre, where the partially Romanesque church of Notre-Dame is found. Behind Rochecorbon a large wine plateau stretches out, and it is possible to drive across this to Vouvray or Vernou-sur-Brenne. However, we recommend instead that you turn back to the Loire quay and follow it in an easterly direction. First you will pass the Musée de la Coiffe et

Château de Noizay
Noizay
℡ 47.52.11.01
This 16th-century castle was builtin the middle of a forest and an ornamental garden. Lovely furnishings with many antiques. The 14 rooms are spacious and very comfortable (starting at around FF 650). In the restaurant the cuisine is based on regional ingredients and is creative. Menus start at around FF 160.

RESTAURANTS
Auberge des Belles Rives
Rochecorbon
℡ 47.52.52.97
On the quay, with a terrace at the rear (where you may dine when the weather is nice). Carefully prepared cuisine at very reasonable prices. The Menu du Terroir costs about FF 100.
Auberge La Cave Martin
Vouvray
℡ 47.52.62.18
Situated at the end of La Vallée Coquette, past the co-operative, on the edge of the wine plateau. Tasty dishes

successful sparkling wine Blanc Foussy.
Domaine la Saboterie Delicious Demi-Sec and Moelleux. The owner teaches at the viniculture school.
Société Tourangelle de Vins Fins Makes sparkling Touraine wines with the Beauvolage label (nice rosé and red).
VERNOU-SUR-BRENNE

Gilles Champion Among others a charming Demi-Sec.
Domaine de Clérambault It also sells wine from Domaine des Perruches.
Domaine de la Mabillière
Eliane Métivier Good Vouvray Sec, Brut and Moelleux. Many old vines.
François Pinon Very old wine estate.

(often using duck), pleasing prices (menus under FF 100) and friendly service.

Le Grand Vatel
Vouvray
℗ 47.52.74.52
Impressive selection of Loire wines and a rather regal cuisine with good fish and meat dishes. Menus start at around FF 130. A few pleasant hotel rooms starting at about FF 300 (often with half-board).

L'Oubliette
Rochecorbon
℗ 47.52.50.49
Thanks to the boss, who cooks inventively, this is a well-known restaurant and a recommended place to eat. Classic dishes, such as *coq au vin*, are often included in the inexpensive weekly menu. Normal menus start around FF 175.

TOURIST TIPS
• A Route du Vouvray/Circuit des Vignobles runs through the vineyards.
• In the season, cave walks are organised in Rochecorbon.

Broderies de Touraine. In a hall here dozens of lace bonnets are exhibited. After *Phylloxera* had destroyed the vineyards of Vouvray, local women began to make these bonnets in order to earn money. Further along the quay a road runs upwards to Château de Moncontour, a building that originated in the 15th century. Formerly there were tourist attractions in and around the castle (such as a wine museum) but it is now closed to visitors. Wine is still made in the cellars below it, however. *Vouvray* itself consists of narrow, often sloping streets which lead up to the wine plateau. The oldest part of the church of Notre-Dame is 13th-century; two of its chapels are carved out of the cliff. In the vicinity of the church is since 1990 a museum, called L'Espace de la Vigne et du Vin, with old wine apparatus, an old kitchen, a collection of old photos (not related to wine) and other items. The guided tour concludes with a wine tasting. From

Vouvray has its own type of glass, here on a façade.

VOUVRAY
Domaine des Aubuisières Top quality.
Caves des Producteurs La Vallée Coquette An important co-operative with high standards.
Clos Baudoin Large estate, excellent wines. Already in operation in the 15th century.

Didier Champalou Makes a lot of Moelleux (such as the C.C.).
Régis Fortineau Among others a good Vieilles Vignes.
Domaine Freslier Moelleux, Pétillant.
Château Gaudrelle Much wood fermentation.
Domaine Huet/Le Haut-Lieu A leading

Vouvray it is not far to *Vernou-sur-Brenne*, a pleasant village built in a valley where Gallic-Roman ruins can be found (rue Aristide-Briand). The church de la Sainte-Trinité (where a market takes place on Thursdays) is 12th-century. A beautiful road runs to *Noizay*. The 16th-century castle here is now a luxurious hotel and the small church of Saint-Prix has an 11th-century nave and a pietà from the 16th century. In Noizay, take the D 78 to *Chançay*. You will find old buildings dating from the 16th century here, including the remains of the Château de Valmer. From Chançay you can return to Vouvray and the bank of the Loire by way of Vernou-sur-Brenne.

The church in Noizay.

- In the Moulin de Touvoie near Rochecorbon, Jean Cocteau filmed his La Belle et la Bête.
- Near Vouvray's church is a monument devoted to Charles Bordes, who was born here in 1863 and who revived Gregorian music.

wine estate that uses biological cultivation. Marvellous wines.
Daniel Jarry Apart from being a successful wine producer, he is also a bottle collector.
Jean-Pierre Laisement Often crowned.
Daniel Alias Vinifies his fruit-rich Clos du Petit-Mont separately.

RELATED TO WINE
- In the first week of November Vouvray celebrates the festival of La Bernache for a whole day.
- Wine fairs in Vouvray on the last Saturday in January and in the middle of August.

HOTEL
Hôtel de la Ville
Montlouis-sur-Loire
© 47.50.84.84
Peaceful, rural hotel in
the heart of the village.
Around 30 rooms

MONTLOUIS

The winegrowers of Montlouis, an area on the south bank of the Loire, across from Vouvray, have tried to form an affiliation with Vouvray but without success. This is easily explained. It is because similar wines are made in both areas from the chenin blanc, although that of Montlouis tastes somewhat less full and usually ripens slightly quicker. In Montlouis they also make a bone-dry Sec, as well as Demi-Sec, Moelleux, sparkling Brut and Pétillant. The district between the Loire and the Cher contains only one-sixth of Vouvray's area of vineyard and is named after Montlouis-sur-Loire. This village, which is partially sited on a hill, can be reached by way of Tours or Amboise. The road from Amboise is particularly beautiful and sometimes runs close by the Loire. On the way you will pass *Lussault-sur-Loire*, where the church has a remarkable nave and a hemisperical apse, and *Huisseau*, which also

Château de la Bourdaisière.

starting at about FF 275. In the unpretentiously decorated restaurant you can eat well: tasty, rather uncomplicated dishes such as *confit de canard grillé* and *friture de Loire*. Menus begin under FF 100 but the one at around FF 150 offers particularly good value for money.

TOURIST TIPS
• Sometimes a jazz festival is organised in September in Montlouis.
• As in Vouvray, the festival of La Bernache, the young wine, is celebrated

Tasting in the Cave Touristique.

RECOMMENDED PRODUCERS
HUISSEAU
Claude Levasseur Delicious Pétillant and Brut. Subtle Moelleux, ripened in wood.
Dominique Moyer Many old vines and old vintages. Beautiful Moelleux.
Domaine de la Taille aux Loups

Wines with their own style (lots of wood).
MONTLOUIS-SUR-LOIRE
Domaine de Bodet
Yves et François Chidaine They bottle the wines of Clos Habert and Clos du Breuil.
Domaine René-Pierre Dardeau Very old family estate. Delightful Moelleux.

View in Montlouis-sur-Loire.

has an old church and, near the entrance to *Montlouis-sur-Loire,* the co-operative with cellars in caves.

here in November.
- The villages are situated at the feet of plateaus on which vineyards are planted. It is worth the effort to make a trip through these elevated vineyards.
- Four walking routes have been set out around Montlouis.

Near the turn-off to the centre of Montlouis is the Cave Touristique, where old wine tools are exhibited and 25 producers sell a selection of their wines. In the village you will find the church of Saint-Laurent, which was built in the 12th and 13th centuries on the ruins of a 6th-century chapel. Additional parts were built on until the 19th century. The presbytry next door is 16th-century. A perfect, restored, 16th-century castle, which can be visited, stands just outside Montlouis and is called the Château de la Bourdaisière. Gabrielle d'Estrées, who later became the mistress of Henry IV, was born here in 1565. In the 55-hectare park there are about 100 different tree species. The interior contains marvellously furnished Renaissance salons. Next to the complex is a riding school. To the east of Montlouis lies *Saint-Martin-le-Beau.* The Vikings were defeated here in 838: the 'beau' derives from 'bello' (war). In the centre there are sloping streets with old houses and a 12th-century church.

Montlouis-sur-Loire.

George Fradin Still and sparkling wines.
Domaine de la Milletière
G.A.E.C. de Saint-Julien They give their wines much time.
SAINT-MARTIN-LE-BEAU
Berger Frères Absolutely reliable, with a delicious Brut and various still wines.
Domaine Delétang Top quality.

Maurice Lelarge For his Moelleux.
Domaine des Tourtenelles Demi-Sec.

RELATED TO WINE
- Last weekend in April: wine fair in Montlouis-sur-Loire.

🏨 **HOTELS**

Le Choiseul
Amboise
✆ 47.30.45.45
Luxurious and very comfortable hotel complex, spread over various buildings, just east of the castle, along the Loire. Around 30 rooms, starting at about FF 500. Excellent, refined cuisine. Menus start at around FF 250. Swimming pool.

Hôtel du Parc
Amboise
✆ 47.57.06.93
Almost 20 rooms in the main building and an annexe, with a small park at the rear. Rural comfort, which varies with each room and is sometimes very simple. Prices start at around FF 250. Its restaurant has a pleasant, unpretentious menu of four courses for about FF 150. Friendly service.

Château de Pray
Chargé
✆ 47.57.23.67
Here, you lodge in a small, 16th-century castle, surrounded by a park. Prices for the 15 rooms begin around FF 600. It has its own restaurant with menus starting at about FF 200.

TOURAINE-AMBOISE

The small wine area of Touraine-Amboise is situated on both the north and the south banks of the Loire, in the surroundings of Amboise. This cosy, provincial city extends to the foot of the castle, which was built in the 15th century on the foundations of a medieval fortress. It was Charles VIII who began the building. He never lived to see the castle finished, however, because in 1498 he bumped his head against a low gateway (on his way to play fives in the moat) and died shortly afterwards. The work was carried on by Louis XII (who also married Charles's widow Anne of Brittany) and afterwards by Francis I. The latter organised large banquets here and also convinced Leonardo da Vinci to come to Amboise. The Italian genius died in the city three years later, in 1519. Only one-fifth of the castle built by Francis I still remains. The rest was razed in the 17th and 19th centuries. The castle served for a long time as the state prison. The kings abandoned Amboise after

Clos Lucé, where da Vinci stayed.

Francis II executed Huguenots there in 1560. One of the most beautiful buildings still remaining is

🛢 **RECOMMENDED PRODUCERS**
AMBOISE
Lycée Viticole d'Amboise The students acquire experience of the Domaine de la Gabillière, whose various wines – dry white, semi-sweet, Crémant de Loire, red Cuvée François I – are of excellent quality (route de Bléré).

Hubert Denay Small, hard-working estate that produces various wines, including a firm red Cot (Le Breuil).
CANGEY
Catherine Moreau Old family estate that is dynamically run. Elegant Cuvée François Ier, a Gamay that has the aroma of small, red fruits and dry, as well as

the chapel of Saint-Hubert. It was built in the Flamboyant-Gothic style; the fine statuary runs over on to the ceiling. One of the two remaining wings is the Logis du Roi, by the Loire. You will find beautiful furniture here from various periods. The Tours des Minimes has a diameter of about 20 metres and allowed horses to come from the city to the inner courtyard of the castle. The glorious past of the castle, which was actually more of a royal palace, comes to life during the impressive sound and light show that is held in the season, involving over 400 actors. Recollections of Leonardo da Vinci are tastefully kept alive in

The castle of Amboise.

the Clos Lucé, the 15th-century mansion where he lived and worked. There are 40 scale models of his inventions. Amboise also has an interesting postal museum, while in the city hall there is a museum devoted to the history of the city. In the street across from the castle entrance is La Maison Enchantée, where 200 mechanical dolls depict about 20 historical scenes. Along the Loire dam is a striking fountain by Max Ernst (1968) and, in the direction of Bléré, the 44-metre-high Pagode de Chanteloup can be visited and climbed. This curious, oriental-looking tower is the only remant of a castle that once stood here.

Half-board is mandatory in the season.

RESTAURANTS
L'Aubinière
Saint-Ouen-les-Vignes
© 47.30.15.29
The village is situated within the wine area of Touraine-Amboise. The restaurant received its first Michelin star in 1992. Inexpensive lunch menu during the week. Normal menus start at around FF 250. Taste the pike in Touraine-

semi-dry, white wines.
LIMERAY
Domaine Catroux
Domaine Dutertre Very active property, strongly focused on the reception of visitors, with a large cellar, small museum, a charming, small courtyard and superior wines, including the semi-sweet

white Les Menates, the dry Clos du Pavillon, various reds and a Gamay rosé.
Jean et François Péquin Both the rosé Cuvée François Ier and the semi-sweet white have ripening potential.
Domaine de la Prévôte
MOSNES
Domaine Frissant/Domaine des

Mesland.

Auberge de Launay
Limeray
☏ 47.30.16.82
Pleasant place to eat on the n N 152. Delicious fish dishes with much flavour and exquisite desserts. When the weather is nice you eat outside. There are also a few hotel rooms and a swimming pool.

Le Manoir Saint-Thomas
Amboise
☏ 47.57.22.52
On the place Richelieu, where his statue also stands. The décor is Renaissance and there is a small park around the building. They offer an à la carte menu with fixed prices for the various categories of dishes and there is a good menu for around FF 300. Very good cuisine in which exotic ingredients feature.

TOURIST TIPS
• In Amboise there is a large market (on the quay, west side) on Friday and Sunday mornings.
• Just past Cangey (near Limeray) is the menhir of Moulin de Lée.

Other wine municipalities on the south bank are *Chargé* (there are paintings by the 18th-century artist Guérize in the city hall) and *Mosnes* (Romanesque church). On the north bank *Pocé-sur-Cisse* has a 15th-century castle where, formerly, an iron foundry was sited. On the way to *Limeray* you will come across the ruins of a Cistercian abbey (1209), while, in the weatherbeaten, grey church of the village itself, there are a few statues from the 15th and 16th centuries. The wines of Touraine-Amboise are mainly red. The most complete carry the name Cuvée François Ier and are made from cabernet, cot (malbec) and gamay. The white wines can taste dry as well as semi-sweet, and are related to those of nearby Vouvray and Montlouis.

The main street of Limeray.

Barricôts The wines of this property have repeatedly been crowned. The reds in particular have much merit.

RELATED TO WINE
• Amboise has wine fairs at Easter and on 15 August.
• Near to the entrance of the castle of

Amboise, Guy Saget has a wine tasting and selling room. He is a winegrower from the area of Pouilly-Fumé, who also manages a property in Touraine-Mesland.

TOURAINE-MESLAND

The area of Touraine-Mesland is somewhat larger than that of the neighbouring Touraine-Amboise. The accent of its production tends slightly more towards red wine, with the gamay in the leading role. The vineyards stretch out along the north bank of the Loire. Mesland and Onzain are the most important municipalities. The landscape is peaceful; the grapevines grow on plateaus that are fed by small river valleys with meadows and thickets. *Mesland* is a peaceful hill village. The most important sight is a small Romanesque church from the 11th century. This has statuary inside and a 12th-century baptismal font. *Onzain* has a church from the 11th and 12th centuries; it was restored in the 15th. Along the rue de L'Ecrevissière lie the remains of a castle

built around 1183. *Chouzy-sur-Cisse*, east of Onzain, has, within its municipality (north side), the ruins of the de la Guiche abbey. Joan of Arc is said to have taken refuge in the Manoir de Laleu on 24 April 1429.

The village of Mesland.

RECOMMENDED PRODUCERS
MESLAND
Domaine d'Artois Property of the Saget family from Pouilly-sur-Loire. Good wines.
Domaine Brossillon Reliable.
Clos Château Gaillard Excellent.
MONTEAUX
Clos de la Briderie Also a small museum.
ONZAIN
Domaine du Chemin de Rabelais

RELATED TO WINE
• Onzain celebrates a fair on the Sunday after Easter.

HOTELS
Domaine des Hauts de Loire
Onzain
℗ 54.20.72.57
Stately, 17th-century building with about 30 luxurious rooms starting at around FF 550. The restaurant has class. Menus start at about FF 230. Swimming pool, tennis court.
Château des Tertres
Onzain
℗ 54.20.83.88
Charming hotel in a small castle on a hill. About 20 pleasant rooms starting at around FF 300. No restaurant.

RESTAURANTS
Pont d'Ouchet
Onzain
℗ 54.20.70.33
Drastically altered at the end of 1992. Regional dishes and wines. Menus start at around FF 120. It also has a bar, tearoom and 11 simple rooms. In the season half-board is mandatory.

TOURIST TIPS
• Onzain has a golf course with a hotel (54.20.49.00).

BLOIS

In regard to size and population, Blois is considerably smaller than the other four large cities of the Loire area – Angers, Bourges, Nantes and Orléans – but in attractiveness it is definitely not inferior. This, to a large extent, is due to its castle, which is situated on a hill in the centre and is an interesting blend of four architectural styles. The medieval period (13th century) is represented by the free-standing Tour du Foix and the arched Salle des Etats Généraux, a large meeting hall. The intermediary period between Gothic and Renaissance (end 15th, beginning 16th century) is seen in the Louis XII wing (where you will find the entrance as well as the Musée des Beaux-Arts), while the pure

The famous castle stairs.

Renaissance style (16th century) is brilliantly presented in the Francis I wing. The other side, where there is a spacious inner courtyard, is dominated by an octagonal, open, spiral staircase with marvellous statuary. Inside, is the apartment of Catherine de Médicis, which has a richly decorated cabinet with numerous small, secret drawers. You can also visit an archaeological museum in this wing, as well as a room devoted to one of the earliest masters of magic, Jean-Eugène Robert-Houdini (1805-71) who was born in Blois. The Classical architectural style (17th century) is present in the form of the Gaston of Orléans wing. Many princes and princesses have lived in the castle. A bloody event occurred in 1588, when Henry III, who was afraid of dethronement, had the powerful duke Henry de Guise murdered here. From the castle terrace there is a beautiful view across ancient Blois and the Loire. The district is very charming, with narrow streets, small stairways and half-timbered houses. The former minster of Saint-Nicolas is also situated here, of which the oldest parts, such as the choir, date from the 12th century. Further east in the city centre is the cathedral of Saint-Louis, which has a large, ancient crypt (10th-century). Behind the cathedral is the city hall, which is housed in a former episcopal palace dating from the 18th century. Here there is a flower garden that also offers a view across the old city and the river valley.

HOTELS

Château du Breuil
Cheverny
✆ 54.44.20.20
Around 20 stylish rooms in a 15th- to 18th-century castle set in the middle of a forest. Prices start at about FF 550. Very good cuisine. Menus start at around FF 200.

La Clé des Champs
Chitenay
✆ 54.70.42.03
Peacefully situated in a small park. Ten pleasant, simple rooms starting at around FF 120. The cuisine in the restaurant is traditional. Menus start at around FF 140.

Le Saint-Florent
Mont-près-Chambord
✆ 54.70.81.00
Around 15 modern rooms in a hotel on the edge of a forest. Prices start at around FF 180. It is also a restaurant.

Hôtel Saint-Michel
Chambord
✆ 54.20.31.31
In the castle park. About 40 comfortable, peaceful rooms starting at around FF 200. In its restaurant you can eat well with menus costing about FF 120 each.

The perfectly symmetrical castle.

CHEVERNY

Directly to the south of Blois, 20 municipalities form the wine area of Cheverny. The limited production consists of fresh, cheerful white wines and sympathetic reds, which are made from a single grape variety (such as gamay, pinot noir, cot or a cabernet) as well as from various varieties. The heart of the region consists of *Cour-Cheverny* and bordering *Cheverny*. In the latter village there is a prominent castle, which was finished in 1634 and built on the foundations of a medieval fortress. Château de Cheverny is private property and stands on land that has belonged to the same family for centuries. The castle, built from grey-white Bourré stone, has a perfectly symmetrical form. The façade (without both of the corner towers) inspired cartoonist Hergé to create Marlinspike castle in the Tintin books. On entering, visitors receive a brochure in

RECOMMENDED PRODUCERS
CELLETTES
G.A.E.C. Dorléans-Ferrand/Domaine de la Gaudronnière Rather large estate with various white and red wines of good quality.
CHEVERNY
François Gazin A white Romorantin

from old vines and a fruity Gamay. The vineyard is on the castle estate.
Domaine Tessier Exquisite Romorantin, pure Sauvignon, surprising Gamay, charming Pinot Noir.
CORMERAY
Domaine de la Plante d'Or Among other wines a successful Romorantin.

their own language and are then allowed to walk around alone. The rooms, salons and halls are marvellously furnished with antique furniture. Particularly impressive is the armoury with its suits of armour and weapons from the 15th and 16th centuries and its marvellous 17th-century wall tapestry. Next to it is the richly decorated royal chamber, where Henry IV once slept. In the annexe there is a trophy room with about 2,000 deer antlers, an orangery and kennels for a pack of 70 hounds (fed at the end of the afternoon). Hunting scenes from the past are brought to life around the castle in a summer sound and light show.

There is beautiful furniture in the castle.

Another, much smaller, castle in the municipality of Cheverny is that of Troussay. It has an intimate Renaissance interior of great beauty and, in an annexe, a museum devoted to the Sologne region. By driving in a southwesterly direction along the D 52, you come into *Fougères-sur-Bièvre*. The castle here has a square keep from the 11th century, while, in the main building, you can admire enormous fireplaces and beautiful woodcarving. There are also a few castles to the north of Cheverny. Beauregard, in the municipality of *Celettes,* is surrounded by a large park and is built in the Renaissance style. Inside

Hôtel des 3 Marchands
Cour-Cheverny
℡ 54.79.96.44
About 40 rooms of varying comfort. The simplest are spartanly furnished. Prices start at around FF 220. Private, spacious parking lot. Somewhat rustic restaurant where you can dine pleasantly. For around FF 150 you can enjoy a good three-course meal.

COUR-CHEVERNY
Domaine de la Désoucherie Strong in both white and red wines.
G.A.E.C. Givierge Père & Fils/Clos de l'Aumônière Reliable.
Domaine des Huards The largest private wine estate. Michel Gendrier makes, among others, a superb Romorantin.

FOUGERES-SUR-BIEVRE
Domaine de Salvard Attractive red wines and a lively Sauvignon.

FRESNES
Domaine Sauger & Fils Various quality wines, including Romorantin, Sauvignon and red Cabernet.

RESTAURANTS
La Pousse Rapière
Cheverny
℡ 54.79.94.23
Rural inn near the castle entrance. Cuisine from the southwest. Wild game when in season and a plat du jour (such as *pot au feu*) for less than FF 100.

Le Relais de Bracieux
Bracieux
℡ 54.46.41.22
The best place to eat in the region. On the menu there are always dishes made with Loire wines, while in the cellar 30,000 bottles are kept. Elegant interior. Menus start at around FF 300.

TOURIST TIPS
• Cheverny has a golf course.
• Note the beautiful, little old church of Cheverny, across from the castle entrance.
• In Cour-Cheverny there is a market on Tuesdays.

there are 363 historical portraits and, in one of the rooms, the floor is made of Delft ceramic tiles which show an army on the march at the time of Louis XIII. In the 16th-century castle of Villesavin, near *Bracieux*, a collection of carriages may be seen. Finally there is the castle of *Chambord*, less than a ten-minute drive from Bracieux. Its 440 rooms, 365 chimneys and 84 staircases make it the largest castle of the Loire. Commissioned by Francis I in the 16th century, 1,800 labourers worked on it for 15 years and even then it was not finished. Apart from the marvellous main staircase, there are reminders of the occupants, who were often of royal blood, and its history comes to life in a summer sound and light show. According to tradition, it was Francis I who brought the romorantin grape to the area in 1519, nowadays a rare white variety that gives a very dry, lively wine with a curious, somewhat floral aroma and ripening potential.

Panel with wine motif in Cheverny's castle.

MONT-PRES-CHAMBORD
Co-operative

RELATED TO WINE
• In the sales room of Château de Cheverny wine is sold that has been selected by the owner himself. The quality is good.

ORLÉANAIS

That wine has been made around Orléans for centuries is shown, among other things, by the grape motif on one of the southern towers of the Georges V bridge which connects the centre of Orléans to the other bank. Under Charlemagne a vineyard was created not far from the city and Francis I commissioned the clearing of part of the forest of Orléans in order to plant grape-vines. Most of the present 150 hectares of vineyards are situated to the southwest of Orléans, between Saint-Hilaire-Saint-Mesmin and Cléry-Saint-André. They are planted with black

The cathedral of Orléans.

grapes such as pinot meunier (from which the somewhat earthy Gris Meunier is made), pinot noir (sometimes called auvernat rouge) and cabernets, while often surprisingly good white wines are made from the chardonnay (auvernat blanc). Most of the winegrowers live in *Mareau-aux-Prés*, a rather colourless transit village. Only the private wine museum (700 objects) of the Clos de Saint-Fiacre producer deserves a visit. *Cléry-Saint-André*, slightly to the south, has an impressive basilica in the Flamboyant style. Louis XI often went there to pray and he is buried there along with his wife. Henry II and Henry III also

HOTELS
L'Abbaye
Beaugency
✆ 38.44.67.35
About 20 distinguished rooms. A number of them offer a view across the Loire. There is also a terrace on the river quay. Prices start at around FF 450. In their restaurant menus start at about FF 200.
L'Ecu de Bretagne
Beaugency
✆ 38.44.67.60

RECOMMENDED PRODUCERS
MAREAU-AUX-PRÉS
Co-operative This firm, which works under the name of Les Vignerons de la Grand'Maison, has about 70 members. Among the better wines are the almost rosé-like Gris Meunier and the red Cabernet.

Jacky Legroux Nice red and rosé
G.A.E.C. Clos de Saint-Fiacre This is the most trend-setting private wine firm in the Orléanais. The best wine from the range is the Auvernat Blanc/Chardonnay, which is juicy and has quite a bit of fruit. The red wines (some wood-ripened) and the rosé are also worth discovering. The

Try to get a room at the rear of the main building, because the modern annexe is much less cosy. Around 20 rooms, starting at about FF 150. A restaurant decorated with a lot of wood, that is rich in ambiance. Menus start around FF 120.

Hôtel de la Sologne
Beaugency
✆ 38.44.50.27
A perfect rural hotel situated on a charming little square between the keep and the Tour Saint-Firmin. Classically furnished rooms (about 15, starting at around FF 150) and friendly service. No restaurant.

RESTAURANT
L'Escale du Port-Arthur
Saint-Hilaire-Saint-Mesmin
✆ 38.76.30.36
Rural dishes are prepared here with care and products from Clos de Saint-Fiacre are on the wine list. Menus start at around FF 110. It is also a hotel.

In the heart of Beaugency.

visited it. It is not far from Cléry-Saint-André to *Beaugency.* This city can be reached by way of a long, still partially 16th-century, arched bridge. The village centre is medieval, charming and colourful. Near the Loire quay is the Tour du Diable, a former defensive construction. A small winding street runs upwards along it to the place Dunois. This is dominated by the remains of an enormous, rectangular keep from the 11th century. Beside it is a small 15th-century castle, in which the Musée Régional de l'Orléanais has been housed (many regional works of art, scale models and a room devoted to winegrowing). On the square you will also see the former minster of Notre-Dame (12th-century in origin) and, just further up, the high Tour Saint-Firmin (16th-century clock tower) and a statue of Joan of Arc.

One of the best wine producers.

firm has its own wine museum and, apart from wine, also sells regional products.

OLIVET
Covifruit The suburb of Olivet is situated to the south of Orléans and on the south bank of the Loiret. Covifruit, a co-operative that also produces a lot of fruit, brings a number of pleasant wines on to the market, in white, red and rosé. The unattractive-looking building is situated in a residential area (rue du Pressoir-Tonneau; crossing the Loiret bridge when coming from Orléans, take the road to the right, at the T-junction by the town hall turn right, then take the first street left).

ORLÉANS

The city of Orléans stands on the northernmost point of the Loire and has twice played a leading role in attempts to drive occupying forces out of the country. This occurred for the first time in 52 BC, when a rebellion of the Gauls against the Roman occupation began in Orléans, which was then called Genabum. A year later this revolution was crushed near Alésia. The second time was in 1429, when Joan of Arc drove off the English army which was storming Orléans. She had received permission to do this from Charles VII, who resided in Chinon. There were not enough English soldiers to surround the entire city, so the 17-year-old shepherdess from Lorraine was able to enter Orléans without difficulty. This took place on 29 April. In the following days the French fought evermore fiercely with the English. Joan was wounded but carried on heroically. On 8 May the English retreated, which was the beginning of their departure from the whole of France. The inhabitants of Orléans still celebrate this liberation annually on that day, with a high mass in the morning and a long procession in the afternoon. It goes without saying that visitors to Orléans are reminded of Joan of Arc in many other ways. She was canonised in 1920. You often come across her name and image. Thus, there is a large statue of the Maid of Orléans on the place du Martroi. She sits on a horse that rises from a plinth on which important episodes from her life are depicted in relief. This square is in the heart of the city and is one of the most beautiful and charming parts. From the place du Martroi it is a walk of 400 metres, in an easterly direction, to the Hôtel Groslot, the former city hall. In front of this 16th-century brick building is another statue of Joan of Arc. Inside you may visit salons, while, behind the building, is a garden containing the remains of the 15th-century chapel of Saint-Jacques. The Hôtel Groslot is built almost in the shadow of the cathedral de la Sainte-Croix. It was set on the partially visible foundations of a 4th-century basilica and was largely built in the Gothic style. Both of the 80-metre-high towers taper off gradually and are set on a façade with three large portals and three rose windows. The church treasury is of enormous wealth, including glazed Byzantian medals (11th-century). Naturally, one of the chapels is devoted to Joan of Arc. On the north side of the cathedral is the Musée des Beaux-Arts. This is one of France's most prominent museums. The collection of French paintings from the 17th and 18th centuries is, in particular, extremely

impressive, although there are also paintings from other countries (such as the Dutch masters Van Goyen and Van de Velde). By following the rue Jeanne d'Arc from the cathedral in a westerly direction, you will arrive at place Charles de Gaulle. The Maison Jeanne d'Arc, the (restored) half-timbered house where she stayed, is found here. This building houses a museum that depicts various aspects of her life. Not far from here Orléans earliest history is celebrated in the Musée Historique et Archéologique (place de l'Abbé Desnoyers). To the north of the boulevards that border the old centre is the Musée d'Orléans (rue Marcel Proust). This has, on one hand, a physics collection with dioramas of stuffed mammals and, on the other hand, objects from other civilisations, including the coffin of a Kanak chief from New Caledonia.

Orléans, which already had the status of a university city by 1305, suffered greatly during the Second World War. About 3,000 buildings were entirely destroyed and 8,000 in part. However, enough buildings were spared to give atmosphere to the centre and many of the houses were rebuilt or restored with great care. The present university is situated on the south bank, in the suburb of Orléans La Source. This is also the location of the Parc Floral Source de Loiret. From the beginning of April until the beginning of November, it offers visitors a luxurious wealth of flowers. As well as other flowers, the park has 25,000 irises in 600 varieties (second half of May) and 100,000 roses (second half of June). There is a 17th-century castle in the park where you will find the source of the small Loiret river, which gave its name to the department of which Orléans is the capital.

Statue of Joan of Arc in front of the Hôtel Groslot.

Gien is a centre of glazed pottery.

COTEAUX DU GIENNOIS

Although Coteaux du Giennois is one of the smallest wine areas of the Loire, it stretches out over a substantial distance because the vineyards are situated between Gien and Cosne-sur-Loire, 40 kilometres to the south. Most of the wines are red and come from the gamay but those made from the pinot noir are usually of higher quality. The white grapes are sauvignon and chenin blanc. Some Sauvignons resemble a minor Sancerre, while others taste rather rustic. Above *Gien* rises a sturdy castle, which was built in the 15th century for Anne de Beaujeu, the daughter of Louis XI. It houses a large hunting museum. Next to the castle is the church of Sainte-Jeanne-d'Arc, of which only the towers still date from the 15th century. The rest was lost during the Second World War and was afterwards rebuilt. Joan of Arc visited Gien four times, as is shown

RECOMMENDED PRODUCERS
GIEN
Jean Poupat et Fils Small producer of red, rosé and white (Sauvignon, usually quickly sold out). The wine is made in Briare in stainless steel tanks, while the office and tasting room are situated in Gien (47, rue Georges-Clemenceau).

MÉNÉTEREAU
Jacques Carroué In this hamlet, to the southeast of Cosne, Carroué makes good red and rosé wines from the gamay.
Jean-Paul Nérot Red and rosé.
Langlois Père & Fils The Gamay has good fruit, the Pinot Noir is very correct and the Sauvignon cheerful. They also

by a tile picture on the church wall. By driving in a northerly direction from the square near the church , you come to a *faïencerie*, a factory that makes glazed earthenware. A museum is also housed here. At attractive prices second-rate items and the remains of finished lines are offered for sale.

Cosne-sur-Loire.

RESTAURANT
La Panetière
Cosne-sur-Loire
℃ 86.28.01.04
Outside there is ivy growing on the façade; inside there is a pleasant ambiance. Rather traditional dishes. One of the best menus is around FF 170. Situated on the place de la Pêcherie.

By way of the N 7 it is about half an hour's drive to *Cosne-sur-Loire*. This city is situated at the place where the Nohain flows into the Loire. By means of the place de la Pêcherie (where the city was founded by Gauls) you can drive along the Loire quay. You then drive under the suspension

Gien with its castle and church.

Wrought iron anchor in Cosne-sur-Loire.

TOURIST TIPS
- Cosne's Musée Municipal displays many aspects of the Loire's history and there are also paintings by Chagall and Utrillo.
- In Cosne there is the Romanesque church of Saint-Agnan and the Gothic church of Saint-Jacques.

bridge, which connects Cosne with the other bank, and pass the former iron foundry, where, in the 17th century, 'volcanic fire from hell raged'. Near the shaded car park at the end of the quay there is a large wrought-iron fence which was once the entrance to the foundry. On the quay, in the grass, stands a large 19th-century anchor that was made in Cosne; it weighs 2,580 kilograms.

make a rather earthy Crème de Cassis. The cellars are situated close to the church of Pougny (not far from Cosne).
VILLEMOISON
Jean Jarreau The Pinot Noir that is produced here is one of the very best of the area.
Alain Paulat Believes strongly in the

gamay and tries to make from it a wine that you can keep. The wine usually has a deep colour and a firm taste with a bit of *terroir*. He also makes a little Pinot Noir and a tiny amount of Sauvignon. The village is a ten-minute drive from Cosne.

The castle of Valençay attracts many visitors.

VALENÇAY

In the south the wine area of Valençay borders on Touraine. There is even a question of overlapping, because most of the producers make wines with both of the appellation. The wines of Valençay are mainly red, with a rather light, uncomplicated taste. The Beaujolais gamay grape is planted most; aside from this you will also see, among others, cot (malbec), pinot noir and cabernets. The best white wines are made from sauvignon blanc, chardonnay and chenin blanc. One of the most important wine municipalities is *Meusnes*, not far from Saint-Aignan, Selles-sur-Cher and the southern Cher bank. In Meusnes,

RECOMMENDED PRODUCERS
FONTGUENAND
Co-operative This is the largest producer of Valençay. Apart from nice reds it also has pleasant white wines.
LEYE
F. Jourdain
Jean-François Roy

Robert Vaillant You should taste the Chardonnay.
MEUSNES
Jacky et Philippe Augis A regal series of light, fruity wines from Valençay as well as Touraine.
Hubert Sinson/Domaine de la Maison Blanche One of the best producers of the

aside from an 11th-century church, you will find the Musée Pierre à Fusil. This is devoted to flint (history, tools, weapons), because gigantic amounts of flint were once produced in the village, above all in the 16th century, but also during the Napoleonic Wars. To the south of Meusnes – follow the signs of the Route Touristique et du Vignoble des Coteaux du Cher – are a few hamlets where winegrowers live. On the south bank of *Fontguenand*, a village along the D 956, is the wine co-operative. Then follow a road surrounded by woods to *Valençay*. After a roundabout with a monument, the castle comes into sight. It is a magnificent Renaissance building, which was, for the most part, built in the 16th century but was expanded in the 17th and 18th centuries. The main buildings, which are at right-angles to each other, are flanked by an enormous domed tower. In 1803 the castle was bought by the statesman Talleyrand. Five years later the Spanish King Ferdinand VII, who had been dethroned by Napoleon, was an involuntary guest. Reminders of Talleyrand and the Spanish royal house are still present in the castle, including the writing table that the Frenchman is said to have used in 1815 at the Congress of Vienna. Near the castle there is a zoo and the Musée de l'Automobile, with old cars, motorcycles and accessories.

private theatre.
Médiathel
Valençay
℡ 54.00.38.00
Rather modern complex with more than 50 rooms. Prices start at around FF 260. Restaurant. Swimming pool.

RESTAURANT
Le Chêne Vert
Valençay
℡ 54.00.06.54
You can eat rural dishes inexpensively here (for less than FF 100), sometimes prepared with regional wines. When the weather is good, meals are served on the terrace.

TOURIST TIP
• In the season a sound and light show is held near the Château de Valençay.

The castle also has a zoo.

region, which shows, among others, in its many crowned wines. One of the most delicious Valençays is the Cot.
Jacky Preys This is the largest private winegrower. The red wines are mainly worth attention. A substantial part of the harvest consists of Touraine wines.

RELATED TO WINE
• In the first half of May Valençay usually organises a wine fair.
• During Whitsun there is usually a wine fair in Meusnes.

Château de la Ferté, in the vicinity of Reuilly.

REUILLY

It is possible that, in AD 630, Good King Dagobert gave the abbey of Saint-Denis to *Reuilly*, a village not far to the south of Vierzon. This one doesn't exist anymore, but there is a partially Romanesque church from the 11th century, Le Prieuré, in the village. La Grande Maison was a hospital in former times. Apart from that, there is not much else to see in Reuilly, whose streets slope slightly because it is built on hills. A beautiful building, which can be viewed but not visited, is the Château de la Ferté in the hamlet of the same name (along the D 918 to Issoudun). The château is 17th-century, has pepperpot towers, is surrounded by a square

RECOMMENDED PRODUCERS
LURY-SUR-ARNOU
Olivier Cromwell This is indeed the winegrower's name. If only because of this, his white Reuilly is exported to England.
PREUILLY
Henry Beurdin White Reuilly. Makes a

rosé from the pinot noir.
Jean-Michel Sorbe Delicious rosé and good white, plus red Reuilly.
REUILLY
François Charpentier Enjoys a good name mainly because of his red wine.
Jacques Chassiot Rosé from the pinot noir. Established in La Ferté.

moat and houses a stable (guestrooms will be available in the future). On the west side of Reuilly is the white Château de l'Ormeteau, a former fortress of the Templars, which is surrounded by deciduous trees. Although the village itself gives one no urgent reason for a visit, its wine does, because one of the rarest and most exquisite dry rosés of the Loire area is made here: a rosé from the pinot gris. This has a nimble taste and an amiable bouquet; you seldom see it outside of the region. The white Reuilly can also be a treat. The base for this lively, clear-tasting wine is the sauvignon. It mostly owes its qualities to the very calcareous soil. Finally, there is also a red Reuilly, from the pinot noir. Apart from the village of Reuilly itself, six other municipalities belong to the wine area, including, very confusingly, *Preuilly*.

Cordier is one of the best-known winegrowers.

In the small centre of Reuilly.

RESTAURANT
L'Aubergade
Diou
© 54.49.22.28
Situated past La Ferté. Rustic ambiance and a good cuisine (salad with duck liver and sherry vinegar, fresh wolf-fish, etc.). Menus start at around FF 150.
Le Reuilly
Reuilly
© 54.49.28.15
Pleasant place to eat, with a smart dining room. Regional dishes, such as *feuilleté* made from warm goat's cheese with chives, and young rabbit with mustard are served. Menus start at around FF 100.

TOURIST TIPS
• To the northeast of Vierzon (15 kilometres) there is the La Picardière golf course.

Gérard Cordier One of the stars of this small wine area. Excellent rosé, successful white, good red Reuilly. Cellar in La Ferté.
Claude Lafond Rather large property with a marvellous rosé (from pinot gris and pinot noir), plus a superior white wine.

Guy Malbete Aromatic white wine, tasty red and a charming rosé.
Didier Martin

RELATED TO WINE
• Wine fair at Easter in Reuilly.

RESTAURANT
Le Petit
Raconteur/Au Bon
Vin de Quincy
Quincy
✆ 48.51.30.25
Cafe, tobacconist's and
restaurant near to the
village square. They
serve goat's cheese
with the local wine and
specialities from Savoie
are prepared when
ordered, including
cheese fondue and
raclette.

QUINCY

Viniculture in Quincy, a modest area just to the
northeast of Reuilly, was stimulated in the 14th
century by the monks of Cîteaux. Among others,
the wines were drunk by the archbishops of
nearby Bourges. Almost all the vineyards are
situated within the municipality of *Quincy*, a
village on the south bank of the Cher. It lies
beside the river and on the low hill behind it. All
the local sights are found around a small square
that is partially overgrown with grass. There you
will see the small village church, a weatherbeaten,
sombre-looking castle with high windows and
cream-coloured
shutters (private
property) and the
mairie (in which a
children's school
has been housed).
At various places
in the village
winegrowers
advertise the
presence of cellars
and tasting
rooms.

The castle of Quincy.

In contrast to
Reuilly and many other Loire areas, only one
wine is made in Quincy – a dry white wine made
from the sauvignon grape. It is one of the very
best of its kind. Some types even resemble certain
types of Pouilly-Fumé, but cost much less.

RECOMMENDED PRODUCERS
BRINAY
Domaine Jacques Rouzé Makes a
Quincy from old vines.
QUINCY
Jérôme de la Chaise His best Quincy is
the Vieilles Vignes.
Claude Houssier/Domaine du

Pressoir
Domaine Jaumier The owner, Denis
Jaumier, is well schooled in wine tech-
nique – which can be tasted in his wine.
Domaine Mardon
Domaine Meunier
Maurice Rapin
Bernard Pichard

Vineyard with sauvignon.

Despite this, Quincy enjoys a limited reputation for its rather modest wine production (only one-tenth of Pouilly-Fumé and still a lot less than Sancerre). The grapevines here are often affected by night-frost. That Quincy's wines are of such good quality is partially due to a strongly siliceous vineyard, which drains well. For the most part, these fields are situated on a former bed of the Cher. The only other village that can produce white Quincy is *Brinay*. There are a few fine mansions and you can admire wall paintings in the church.

TOURIST TIPS

- It is a good idea to picnic, with goat's cheese, baguettes and Quincy, on the bank of the Cher on a summer's day.
- On the south bank of Bourges (Lazenay) there is a golf course. Bourges is situated about 20 kilometres away.

The town hall, school and church.

BOURGES

If, by way of Reuilly, Quincy or Menetou-Salon, you come near to
Bourges, you must certainly visit the city. Its most important
monument can be seen from afar: the cathedral of Saint-Etienne,
which rises on a hill above Bourges. Work on this was begun in 1185
and completed in 1324. The interior of the cathedral, which is one of
the largest in the country, is immense. You enter it by way of a side
door or through one of the five asymmetrical portals that decorate the
façade. Inside this Gothic monument, the 13th-century rose windows
are particularly impressive. The cathedral also houses the largest crypt
in France, with marble figures (including that of the duke of Berry).
Diagonally behind the church is the episcopal garden, which was
designed by Le Nôtre in the 17th century. When the weather is fine
you can enjoy a nice walk. From the car park near the cathedral, you
can drive to the other sights but it is better still to walk to them,
because only then is it possible to enjoy to the full the old buildings
(including half-timbered houses) in the centre. To the northwest of

Cathedral window.

the cathedral is the palace of Jacques
Coeur, minister of finance under Charles
VII, which is surrounded by houses. At
that time he was the richest man in France
and, apart from the palace, owned a
number of magnificent castles. By the
palace La Route Jacques Coeur has been
set out. The palace in Bourges is a
marvellous example of Gothic
architecture. Approximately 20 rooms and
salons, which can all be visited, clearly
demonstrate the incredible wealth of the
builder. Close to the palace is the Musée
du Berry, which is not only devoted to
regional artistic works and archaeological
finds, but also exhibits Italian and Flemish
paintings. The museum is housed in a 16th-century building, the
Hôtel Cujas. In another fine building, Hôtel Lallemant (east of the
palace), there is the Musée des Arts Décoratifs, with beautiful
furniture and a room full of games and toys dating from the 17th
century.

RESTAURANTS
Chez Thérése
Morogues
✆ 48.64.41.81
A bar with a simple
restaurant next to it,
where you can eat
regional dishes for way
below FF 100. Also
omelettes, *charcuterie*,
goat's cheese.
L'Zibb/A la vieille
Auberge
Menetou-Salon
✆ 48.64.81.20
At the top corner of the
village square. Usually
no menu. You take your
place and regale
yourself with regional
dishes plus the local
wine. On Sunday
afternoon it is crowded.
For FF 100 you can enjoy
an ample meal.

Château de Maupas, near Morogues.

MENETOU-SALON

Between Bourges and Sancerre the quiet
landscape of meadows, fields and thickets is now
and then interrupted by vineyards. The reason
for this is that the small wine area of Menetou-
Salon is found here but is spread out over a dozen
municipalities. It makes white wines from the
sauvignon grape and red and rosé wines from the
pinot noir, as does Sancerre. Thus Menetou-
Salon's wines closely resemble
those of Sancerre, although the
white often has more charm, but
less volume and depth, while the
reds are usually fuller and the
rosés often at least as good.
Menetou-Salon is by far the most
important wine municipality.
The first grapevines were planted
here by monks in 1190. Behind

Menetou-Salon lies partly in a valley.

RECOMMENDED PRODUCERS
MENETOU-SALON
Domaine de Châteno/Caves Clément
Old family estate and one of Menetou-
Salon's largest producers. The white
wines in particular – usually wood-
ripened – have a lot of quality. They also
make attractive rosé and red wines.

Various subsidiary brands, such as Gérard
de la Farge. It is situated in the hamlet of
Les Faucards.
G. Chavet & Fils The cellars are situated
on a hill just to the south of the village.
Delicious rosé, white and red Menetou-
Salon. It also produces apples and other
fruit, plus fruit juices.

the church a rectangular square runs upwards against a slope. On this square there are a few cafes and restaurants, as well as the Caveau des Vignerons, a tasting and sales room owned by the collective producers. Near to the square is the entrance to the castle of Menetou-Salon. This magnificent castle was the property of Jacques Coeur. After the French Revolution it began to deteriorate but in the last century it was entirely restored by Prince Auguste d'Arenberg, who also collected marvellous wall tapestries, paintings and furniture in the castle, as well as two libraries. Visitors can also view a saddle room and a collection of antique cars.

Church tower of Menetou-Salon.

Tourist tips

• If L'Zibb is full, walk to the Café du Parc across the street, where, for less than FF 100, you will be served a decent meal.

From Menetou-Salon a pleasant road runs to Morogues. Just past the hamlet of Les Faucards, there is a marvellous view and just before Morogues you can visit the Château de Maupas, which has belonged to the same family since 1688. There you will find royal relics, gobelins, fine furniture and, along the large staircase, 887 plates from the 17th, 18th and 19th centuries. In *Morogues* there is a weatherbeaten, 14th-century church with fine statuary and a sublime wooden canopy inside. The clock tower is octagonal.

Co-operative Reliable firm, which, apart from various Menetou-Salons, also makes Quincy and Reuilly.
Jean-Paul Gilbert Near the church.
Jacky Rat Situated in Les Faucards.
Domaine Jean Teiller et Fils
Morogues
Domaine Henry Pellé Dynamic property that has done pioneer work in giving Menetou-Salon fame and reputation. Exemplary red, white and rosé wines, including the white Clos des Blanchais from old vines and the aromatic red Morogues. It also makes a fine Sancerres from the Clos de la Croix au Garde (white and red).

HOTELS
L'Esterille
Bué
℡ 48.54.21.78
Situated at a junction on
the rather busy D955.
Around 10 simple
rooms, starting at
FF 180. The most
attractive menu is at
around FF 160. Regional
cuisine with, among
other things, smoked
ham from Sancerre.

SANCERRE

The best known and most produced wine of the upper Loire is Sancerre. It is named after the village that is strategically situated on a 300-metre-high hill near the river. In total, the area of origin consists of 14 municipalities, most of which are sited in valleys and are separated from each other by hills and plateaus. On the south slope of the hills there are generally grapevines, while on the cooler north side and the plateaus, grain is usually grown. The most cultivated grape is the sauvignon blanc. The wine made from it is often distinguished by an aroma of gooseberries in combination with a hint of vegetable (such as asparagus), while the taste is fresh and cheerful, with the same fruity and floral elements. Sancerre is a perfect accompaniment for *fruits de mer* (seafood), asparagus and goat's cheese, which is also locally produced. The only other grape is the pinot noir, which is made into rosé as well as red Sancerre. These can be pleasant and even good wines but qualitatively speaking they seldom reach the level of the white. Due to its location, the village of *Sancerre* has a long and violent history. Julius Caesar probably founded a settlement here (there is a Porte

Château de Sancerre.

RECOMMENDED PRODUCERS
BUÉ
Domaine Auchere Among others, Le Désert is good.
Sylvain Bailly/Domaine Croix Saint Ursin Excellent white wines.
Bailly-Reverdy et Fils Superior white, red and rosé wines, including those of

Domaine de la Mercy-Dieu.
Bernard et Jean-Paul Balland
Domaine Joseph Balland-Chapuis
Dynamic, trend-setting producer of various types of Sancerre, excellent Coteaux du Giennois and Pouilly-Fumé. Also deals in other Loire wines.
Domaine du Carrou

César in the village) but Sancerre did not achieve real importance until the 10th century, when count Thibault of Champagne built the impressive hilltop castle and a community grew up around it. After Thibault the counts of Sancerre were the owners of the fortress. During the religious wars of the 16th century, Sancerre became a Protestant stronghold, which led Charles IX to start a siege in 1573. It lasted seven months. On 19 August Sancerre fell, after which part of the castle was destroyed. In 1621 the violence of war again struck the village. This time the fortress was almost entirely razed to the ground. One tower still remains, the 12th-century Tour des Fiefs, which can be climbed in the afternoons on Sundays and holidays. Despite all the damage of war, Sancerre is nowadays an attractive place with picturesque streets where the oldest buildings date back to the 15th century. Within the network of streets there are a few

Hôtel Panoramic
Sancerre
✆ 48.54.22.44
Modern establishment with almost 60 functional rooms, reasonable space and adequate comfort. Prices start at around FF 250. A number of rooms offer a view across the surrounding landscape. In the *La Tasse d'Argent* restaurant the cuisine is not particularly exciting, but the *salade Sancerroise* is usually tasty. Menus start at around FF 125. Swimming pool.

Les Remparts
Sancerre
✆ 48.54.10.18
At the end of 1992 it was taken over and renovated. In total there are 20 rooms. The interior is plain and offers modern comforts. Starting at around FF 300. In the rustic restaurant the menus begin at around FF 100 (*coq au vin* etc.).

Le Saint-Martin
Sancerre
✆ 48.54.21.11
Twelve adequate rooms starting at around FF 200. Rustic dining room, traditional dishes

The wine and cheese village of Chavignol.

Cellier de la Tour/Bernard et Jean-Marc
Crochet Cheerful white Sancerre.
Chameau-Balland et Fils White and red.
Dominique Crochet
Lucien Crochet One of the biggest local names. Among others, white Le Chêne and Vieilles Vignes.
Pierre Girault
Gérard Millet
Pierre Millet-Roger Le Grand Chemarin.
Gérard Morin For the red.
Lucien Picard For his Grange aux Dîmes.

(such as various sorts of entrecôte). Menus start at around FF 70. There is also a tea salon.

RESTAURANTS
La Bonne Auberge
Chavignol
℡ 48.54.01.66
Come here for an omelette, with or without Crottin de Chavignol, or for goat's cheese with a glass of Sancerre.

On Sancerre's village square.

squares, of which the most important is the place de la Halle. This was formerly an open square, but the central part is now occupied by a modern-looking terrace under which the Office du Tourisme is situated. The square is flanked on all four sides by restaurants, arts and crafts stores and a pâtisserie which sells Croquets de Sancerre made from nougat. Wine stores, including those of the heavily competitive houses of Alphonse Mellot and Joseph Mellot, can be found in a street that runs in a northeasterly direction to the Esplanade Porte César. This offers a delightful viewing point across the Loire to the countryside beyond it, including the vineyards of Pouilly-Fumé. At one side of the esplanade, behind a door and in the middle of a park, is the Château de Sancerre. It dates from 1874 and is the property of the Marnier-Lapostolle family, producers of Grand Marnier liqueur. A vineyard belongs to the castle, from which an elegant Sancerre is made. Back in the village and to the right you will find the small place du Souvenir. To the side of the post office there is another panorama to be enjoyed, this time of the Sancerre area. Two streets run from the place de la Halle. They come out at the 18th-century church of Notre-Dame,

Vincent Pinard Various sorts of Sancerre, including La Clémence and Harmonie.
Clos de la Poussie The white wine comes from a natural amphitheatre. Owned by Cordier.
Jean-Max Roger Energetic winegrower with a number of excellent Sancerres,

such as Le Grand Chemarin, Clos Derveau, Vieilles Vignes. He also makes Menetou-Salon.
CHAUDOUX
Les Celliers Saint-Romble/André Dezat et Fils Top class. Also Pouilly-Fumé.
Michel Girard

which is flanked by a massive belfry dating from 1501. Across from here you can buy another local delicacy, Le Lichou. Somewhat further to the south, in the rue Saint-Père, there is the portal of the former church of Saint-Père-la-None, dating from the 11th century.

From Sancerre a beautiful road, which has many good views, winds to *Ménétréol-sous-Sancerre*. At a corner you pass the modern cellars of Joseph Mellot, and there is a turn-off to the former railway station, nowadays the *La Locomotive* restaurant. Now turn sharply right at the stop sign in

Sancerre's church.

Ménétréol. The road goes upwards once more, past the Les Belles Dames vineyard of Gitton Père & Fils. After passing a forest you will have a beautiful view across Sancerre, with grapevines in the foreground. Now turn left, then immediately right and drive straight through vineyards to the D955. Follow this in a southerly direction until the turn-off to *Bué*. In this chaotic collection of houses some of the finest Sancerres are made. Until the 1970s more goats roamed Bué than people, but 'the cow of the poor' has now, for a large part, disappeared and the inhabitants make

Le Caveau
Bué
℡ 48.54.39.71
Simple place for lunch (grills, goat's cheese), also a bar.

L'Esplanade
Sancerre
℡ 48.54.01.36
Brasserie, also a tea salon, on the place de la Halle. Well-prepared, affordable menus starting at under FF 100 (among other things, *faux-filet* with a sauce from Crottin de Chavignol).

L'Etoile
Saint-Thibault
℡ 48.54.12.15
When the weather is good, you can eat outside on the terrace by the Loire. Traditional cuisine (*coq au vin, matelote d'anguille*). There is a menu for under FF 100.

La Ferme de l'Etang
Ménétréol-sous-Sancerre
℡ 48.54.22.63
Go here for a filling, simple and inexpensive meal on a farm. It is situated on a slope half-way between Sancerre and Ménétréol.

Au Fin Chavignol
Chavignol
℡ 48.54.20.63

André Vatan
CHAVIGNOL
Henri Bourgeois Wine merchant with a lot of land. Pure, fine wines, including Le M.D. de Bourgeois, Etienne Henri and La Bourgeoise. Also Pouilly-Fumé.
Domaine Hubert Brochard Large estate. Taste, among others, the Vieilles

Vignes.
Francis et Paul Cotat
Vincent Delaporte et Fils
CRÉZANCY-EN-SANCERRE
Claude Chevreau
Jean Chotard
Domaine du Colombier/Roger Champault

Rustic ambiance, wines made by the owners and tasty regional dishes, including various salads (with, for example, warm Crottin de Chavignol), *jambon de Sancerre* and omelettes. On cool days an open fire burns. Less than FF 100.

Le Jardin de St. Thibault
Saint-Thibault
☎ 48.54.12.28
Small establishment with a light interior and a small terrace at the rear. Various fish specialities, but also *faux-filet* with Pinot-Noir sauce. There is a menu for less than FF 100.

Auberge Joseph Mellot
Sancerre
☎ 48.54.20.53
Come here for *terrines*, omelettes, goat's cheese and wine from the house. On the place de la Halle. Note the winegrowing tools. You can easily eat here for less than FF 100.

La Locomotive
Sancerre
☎ 48.54.39.71
Situated in the former railway station. Besides

their living only from wine. The soil near Bué is often a combination of small pebbles and porous tufa stone. Among the most famous vineyards are the Clos du Chêne Marchand, Clos du Roy, Le Grand Chemarin and Clos de la Poussie (north side of the village), which is situated in a natural

The area has a wine tour.

amphitheatre. Bué lies in a valley. If you drive through the village up the plateau, you will have a good view across this famous wine municipality. Now, by way of the D923, drive in the direction of Menetou-Ratel and, after a few kilometres, turn off to *Chavignol*, which nestles in a small valley and is not only famous for its wine, but also for its goat's cheese, Crottin de Chavignol. On the village square there once stood an elm tree planted by Henry IV. During the ceremony the king apparently said: 'Chavignol is the best wine I have drunk. If all the people in the kingdom would drink it, there would be no more religious wars.' Unfortunately the elm has disappeared, although there is still a fountain. Nearby are a few restaurants. In La Maison du Vigneron wines from Sancerre and other French areas are sold, and there are various

Paul Millérioux White Clos du Roy, white and red Côte de Champtin.
Jack Pinson/Caves du Prieuré MAIMBRAY
Château de Maimbray White and red.
Domaine de Saint-Romble/Paul Vattan et Fils Also for red Sancerre.
MÉNÉTRÉOL-SOUS-SANCERRE

Gitton Père & Fils This wine estate has undergone a spectacular development. Superior Sancerres (such as Les Romains, Les Belles Dames, Les Herses, Les Cris), marvellous Pouilly-Fumés. The family also makes Coteaux du Giennois and Côtes de Duras (French southwest).
MONTIGNY

tasting and sales rooms in Chavignol, such as that of Henri Bourgeois.

The route continues to *Verdigny*. Near the Auberge du Vigneron there is a small wine museum (moved across the street in 1993). It is a good idea to go a short distance back along the way from Verdigny and then to drive in the

Clos de la Poussie in Bué.

direction of Chavignol, turning right at the junction before this village. This brings you to a nice road that goes first to the hamlet of *Chaudenay* and then to *Maimbray*, where there is a chapel with a curious collection of local saints.

a restaurant it also has a bar, disco, swimming pool and solarium. Simple cuisine: *truite meunière, coq au vin*. Low prices. Terrace.

Saint-Saturnin is dominated by its church.

Henri Natter High class.
SAINT-SATUR
Laporte Merchant with his own land. In the Cave de la Cresle he makes wines such as La Cresle de Laporte and Domaine du Rochoy.
SAINTE-GEMME
Domaine du Nozay

SANCERRE
Domaine les Chasseignes/Foussier
Co-operative One of the best wines is the white Duc de Tarente.
Alphonse Mellot Serious firm with very good wines, such as Domaine de la Moussière and Cuvée Edmond (old vines).
Joseph Mellot Modern firm. The best

Also used for receptions and parties.

La Moussière
Sancerre
℗ 48.54.15.01
Stylish restaurant on the place de la Halle. Affordable regional menus (beginning under FF 100) and wines from Alphonse Mellot, the owner.

Restaurant de La Tour
Sancerre
℗ 48.54.00.81
The best place to dine in the area. There is a quick lunch menu at around FF 100 (fish dishes, dessert, glass of Sancerre), but you can also eat more varied and more surprising dishes in the panorama room. On the place de la Halle.

La Treille
Chavignol
℗ 48.54.12.17
Rural dishes (starting at around FF 100 a menu) are served in a rustic ambiance. You can try cold or warm Crottin, with a glass of Sancerre. Open all day.

Auberge du Vigneron
Verdigny
℗ 48.79.38.68
Sober regional dishes (salads, omelettes, trout, *poulet au*

Sury-en-Vaux surrounded by greenery.

Sury-en-Vaux is the next village. It has a clock tower dating from the 13th century, along with a Bacchus head above a fountain. If you drive one kilometre past the church, on your right there is a good view across the hidden hamlet of Les Giraults. There are now various options for continuing the route. You could go in the direction of *Saint-Gemme*, which has an underground church. On the way to the village you will pass the Domaine du Nozay wine estate. From Sury, by way of the D86, you can reach *Cosne-sur-Loire* within 15 minutes (see

The signpost for Sury-en-Vaux

Sancerre is La Chatellerie.
Château de Sancerre Elegant wine.
Domaine Vacheron White, red, rosé: all of them are excellent.
SURY-EN-VAUX
Domaine des Buissonnes/Christian Lauverjat/Domaine Claude Riffault
VERDIGNY-EN-SANCERRE

Pierre Archambault Situated in the Cave du Clos de la Perrière.
Domaine Daulny (in Chaudenay). Exquisite Clos de Chaudenay.
Fournier Père & Fils White Les Chanvrières. Also Pouilly-Fumé.
Roger Neveu et Fils Clos des Bouffants.
Bernard Reverdy et Fils

Coteaux du Giennois). Just before Cosne, on the west bank, is the small Château de Buranlure, where summer art exhibitions are organised. The third possibility is to go to *Saint-Satur*. In the heart of this rather confusing village there is a 14th-century church that was never completed. It belonged to an abbey that has since disappeared. The clock tower is missing. The interior is worth a visit, if only for the 18th-century ship model that hangs from the ceiling. A large viaduct runs over

Sancerre's Tour des Fiefs.

Saint-Satur. The villages of *Saint-Thibault-sur-Loire* and *Fontenay* belong to the same municipality. The first is situated near a bridge across the Loire. After you have passed the second, going in the direction of Sancerre, half-way up the hill you will come to the Caves de la Mignonne. This is an enormous cave cellar where wine and goat's cheese can be enjoyed on the spot and also bought. It also serves as a regional reception room and as a place for wine exhibitions.

Sancerre) at friendly prices (starting under FF 100). There are also four simple *chambres d'hôte* available.

TOURIST TIPS
- In Saint-Thibault, near to the river, there is an 18-hole golf course. On the course there is a restaurant where you can eat, literally and figuratively, on two levels: below simply, above better . Both floors have a menu for under FF 100. (48.54.11.22.)
- Gilles and Rose-Marie Millet have opened the Foie Gras Sancerrois tasting and sales room in the wine village of Crézancy-en-Sancerre. Open at weekends and on holidays. (48.79.00.48).
- On the first Sunday of August Bué celebrates the festival of the magicians. Many winegrowers walk around in costume.
- About 5 kilometres west of Menetou-Ratel is the Château Boucard, a castle dating from the 15th and 16th centuries.

Reverdy-Ducroux et Fils
Domaine de Saint-Pierre
Domaine des Trois Noyers
Domaine des Villots/Jean Reverdy et Fils

RELATED TO WINE
- At Whitsun there is a three-day wine

fair in Sancerre.
- On the last Sunday of July Verdigny celebrates the Fête des Grappes Nouvelles.
- Last weekend in August: the Foire aux Vins de France in the Caves de la Mignonne, Sancerre.

HOTELS
La Bouteille d'Or
Pouilly-sur-Loire
℃ 86.39.13.84
Almost 30 adequate
rooms starting at around
FF 190. Those in the
annexe on the other side
of the street are less
comfortable. Good
cuisine. Menus begin at
under FF 100.
L'Ecu de France
Pouilly-sur-Loire
℃ 86.39.10.97
Situated in the village
centre. A dozen neat,
though boring, rooms
with TV and good
sanitary facilities.
Starting at around FF
200. Private parking.
Inexpensive restaurant.

POUILLY-FUMÉ

The vineyards of Sancerre and Pouilly-Fumé
have a natural border at the Loire, and at the
same time a striking common factor: in both
areas the sauvignon blanc is mainly cultivated.
From this comes the saying: 'Water divides us,
wine brings us together.' The two wines are not
really similar. As a result of a somewhat different
soil, Pouilly-Fumé usually tastes somewhat fuller
and firmer than Sancerre, often with slightly
more race and refinement. The wine also
generally needs more time to develop. Aside from
Pouilly-Fumé, another white wine, Pouilly-sur-
Loire, is made in the area (which is about three
times smaller than Sancerre). This is a rather
neutral, pleasant thirst-quencher from the
chasselas, a variety that was planted here in the
19th century as a table grape.

The most important municipality in this wine
region is *Pouilly-sur-Loire*, in origin a Roman
settlement (Pauliaca Villa). Records show that

Pouilly-sur-Loire lies right by the river.

wine has been made here since the 7th century. In the 11th century the village was the property of Baron Humbault, who never returned from the First Crusade and left his belongings to the Benedictine monastery of La Charité-sur-Loire. The monks helped viniculture in Pouilly to flourish and would remain the owners of Pouilly until the French Revolution. In the 20th century Pouilly-sur-Loire was, for generations, a transit village along the busy N7. In 1973 the road was re-routed and the village became much more peaceful. On a square between the main street

Le Relais Fleuri
Pouilly-sur-Loire
© 86.39.12.99
About 10 rooms, offering modern comfort but some are rather small. Try to get one at the rear, where you will have a view across the nearby river. Rather rustic, not particularly cosy dining room, where the menus (starting at around FF 100) offer much choice, but only average quality. Terrace.

Wine estate in Les Berthiers.

and the Loire quay is the church of Saint-Pierre, of which the oldest parts date from the 13th century and the most recent from the 16th and 18th centuries. A good route to take in order to explore the vineyards and wine cellars would begin by taking the D 28 in a northeasterly direction and then turning off to Saint-Andelain

RECOMMENDED PRODUCERS
LES BERTHIERS
Domaine des Berthiers/J.C. Dagueneau
Jean-Claude Châtelain
Patrick Goulbois/Domaine les Coques
Serge Dagueneau

Domaine Landrat-Guyollot
Domaine Michot
Michel Redde Along the N7. Large wine estate.
LES LOGES
Paul Figeat Also Pouilly-sur-Loire.
Domaine Jean-Claude Guyot
Pierre Marchand et Fils

Château de Tracy.

RESTAURANT
L'Espérance
Pouilly-sur-Loire
© 86.39.07.69
In this white building on
the street corner, you
can order modern dishes
as well as classic ones.
Many Burgundian
specialities, such as
*cassolette d'oeuf en
meurette* and *potée en
feuilleté*, are on the
menu because Pouilly is
situated in the
Burgundian department
of Nièvre. The least
expensive menu is
about FF 100, but the
more expensive menus
or à la carte are more
interesting. Large wine
selection.

in Le Bouchot; you then come to a large wine plateau with a view of the surrounding countryside. At the foot of the plateau, to the left, is Château du Nozet. Since 1787 this elegant, Renaissance-style castle has been the property of the largest local producer, the De Ladoucette family. *Saint-Andelain*, which stands on a 270-metre-high hill, is known for its spiral clock tower. The church was built by the grandmother of Patrick de Ladoucette in gratitude for the return of her son from the First World War. Between Saint-Andelain and the *route nationale* is the winegrowing hamlet of Les Berthiers, which was probably founded in the Middle Ages. After crossing the N7, you can drive to Bois-Gibault by way of a narrow road and from there to *Tracy*. This former port village has an ancient little church with five remarkable tombs. Château de Tracy, which has been in the hands of the same family for six centuries, is not far from here. It is well cared for and stands in the shadow of a 30-metre-high keep dating from the 15th century. Now drive back to Bois-Gibault and continue to follow the Loire. Soon the signpost for *Les Loges*

Patrice Moreux Among others Loge aux Moines.
Jean Pabiot & Fils
MALTAVERNE
Domaine A. Cailbourdin Three *cuvées*.
POUILLY-SUR-LOIRE
Co-operative Good Vieilles Vignes.
Pascal Jolivet Merchant with superior

Pouilly-Fumé and Sancerre.
De Ladoucette Housed in the Château du Nozet. Wine merchant and producer of Pouilly-Fumé, such as the exquisite Baron de L. Also makes Sancerre, Touraine, Vouvray, Chablis.
Hubert Legrand
Domaine J.M. Masson-Blondelet

Château du Nozet owned by De Ladoucette, the largest producer in the area.

will come into view. This is a winegrowing hamlet which you can reach by way of a railway viaduct. The main street slopes upwards. Behind the hamlet there is a beautiful view across the river. That monks practised winegrowing in Les Loges is proved by a field that is called La Loge aux Moines.

Tourist tips
- In Saint-Laurent-L'Abbaye (north of Pouilly) there is a 12th-century abbey (without a gate, because the Americans took it).
- In the centre of Pouilly you will find the Musée Ernest Guédon, with old wine tools, etc.

Guy Saget Also makes other Loire wines. Best Pouilly-Fumé: Les Roches.
Hervé Seguin Also Pouilly-sur-Loire.
Saint-Andelain
Bouchié-Chatellier/La Renardière
Didier Dagueneau Fantastic wines such as the Pur Sang and Marcel Langoux Silex.

Domaine Renaud-Bossuat et Fils
Tracy-sur-Loire
Château de Tracy

Related to wine
- On 15 August there is a wine fair in Pouilly.

INDEX